Stop Kicks

The Art of Kicking Your Opponent At His Most Vulnerable

Jamming, Obstructing, Stopping, Impaling, Cutting and Preemptive Kicks
From All Martial Arts

By

Marc De Bremaeker

author of Low Kicks and PlyoFlex

Turtle Press   Washington DC

To contact the author or to order additional copies of this book:

Turtle Press
500 N. Washington St #5145
Rockville MD 20849
www.TurtlePress.com

ISBN 978-1-938585-34-0
LCCN 2014012583

Printed in the United States of America

Warning-Disclaimer

This book is designed to provide information on the techniques and skills of kicking and martial arts. It is not the purpose of this book to reprint all the information that is otherwise available to the author, publisher, printer or distributors, but instead to compliment, amplify and supplement other texts. You are urged to read all available material, learn as much as you wish about the subjects covered in this book and tailor the information to your individual needs. Anyone practicing the skills, exercises, drills or techniques presented in this book should be physically healthy enough to do so and have permission from a licensed physician before participating.

Every effort has been made to make this book as complete and accurate as possible. However, there may be mistakes, both typographical and in content. Therefore, this text should be used only as a general guide and not as the ultimate source of information on the subjects presented here in this book on any topic, skill or subject. The purpose of this book is to provide information and entertain. The authors, publisher, printer and distributors shall neither have liability nor responsibility to any person or entity with respect to loss or damages caused, or alleged to have been caused, directly or indirectly, by the information contained in this book. If you do not wish to be bound by the above, you may return this book to the publisher for a full refund.

Please note that the publisher and author of this instructional book are NOT RESPONSIBLE in any manner whatsoever for any injury that may result from practicing the techniques and/or following the instructions given within. Physical and Martial Arts training can be dangerous—both to you and others—if not practiced safely. If you are in doubt as how to proceed or whether your practice is safe, consult with an accredited coach, physical trainer or a trained Martial Art teacher before beginning. Since the physical activities described maybe too strenuous in nature for some readers, it is essential that a physician be consulted prior to any type of training.

Recommended reading, by the same author (martialartkicks@gmail.com):

By the same Editor: TURTLE PRESS (www.turtlepress.com)

"*Low kicks*" (2013)

"*Plyo-Flex Training for Explosive Martial arts kicks*" (2013)

by Tuttle Publishing (www.tuttlepublishing.com)

"*The Essential Book of Martial arts Kicks*" (2010)

Cataloging in Publication data

Bremaeker, Marc de.
  Stop kicks : jamming, obstructing, stopping, impaling, cutting and preemptive kicks from all martial arts : the art of kicking your opponent at his most vulnerable / by Marc De Bremaeker.
    pages cm
  ISBN 978-1-938585-34-0
  1. Martial arts--Kicking. I. Title.
  GV1102.7.K52B75 2014
  796.8--dc23
                                    2014012583

DEDICATION

To Nimrod and Dotan,

A father could only wish to have better sons than those…

Acknowledgements

Without the active support of my wife and life companion, this book would not have come to life. Being an athlete in her own right, she understands the meaning of hard work and dedication.

Special Thanks to my life-long friend and training partner, **Sensei Roy Faige**, for his help and support. Roy is also my co-author of *The Essential Book of Martial Arts Kick*, and his influence and advice is felt in nearly every page of this work.

Thank you to **Ziv Faige, Gil Faige, Shay Levy, Dotan De Bremaeker, Nimrod De Bremaeker** and **Itay Leibovitch** who helped by painstakingly posing for some of the photographs.

Nimrod De Bremaeker

Most photographs have been taken by the author and **Aviva Giveoni**. But special thanks have to be extended to talented **Grace Wong** for the long sessions. Thank you also to professional photographer **Guli Cohen**: some of the photographs in this book have been extracted from the photo sessions he gracefully did for previous volumes.

The drawings in this book are mine. Everything that I have learned about line art, I have done so from professional Illustrator **Shahar Navot**, who illustrated *The Essential Book of Martial Arts Kicks*. Thanks Shahar!

Strength does not come from winning. Your struggles develop your strengths.
When you go through hardships and decide not to surrender, that is strength.

~ Arnold Schwarzenegger

Contents

Foreword to the "Kicks" Series

A goal is not always meant to be reached, it often serves simply as something to aim at.

~ Bruce Lee

This Foreword/Introduction is very similar to that of our previous book in the series 'Low Kicks'. Although there are a few small differences and a little emphasis on Stop Kicks, you can skip this Foreword/Introduction if you have read 'Low Kicks'. It will not bring significant new information and you are free to hop directly to the Stop Kicks Introduction on page 15.

My Martial Arts career started with Judo at age 6. Judo was pretty new Fifty years ago, and a bit mystical in the Western World; a mysterious Oriental Art teaching how to use one's opponent's strength against him was a pretty attractive proposition for a wimpy kid. And the decorum and costume trappings made it a unique selling proposition. That is, until the Kung Fu craze of the Seventies...Bruce Lee et al.

In my opinion, what fascinated the Western masses, and the teen-ager I was then, was mostly the fantastic kicking maneuvers of the fights of these Kung Fu movies. The bulk of the fight scenes were based on spectacular kicking exchanges, the likes of which we had never seen before. We had been conditioned by boxing and the fair-play of Queensbury's rules, and had no idea one could fight like that. It was also the first time most people in Europe and America had seen a well-rounded Martial Art comprising all fighting disciplines: kicking, grappling, striking... *Judo* was nice, but I also wanted to learn to <u>kick</u> like Lee. I took up *Shotokan Karate*, as it was the only one available yet, and the most developed outside of Japan.

Shotokan Karate is very well organized didactically and emphasizes tradition, hard training and basic work. Though it is not an art know for extravagant kicks, I never stopped practicing it, or a Shotokan-derived style, during all my athletic years. In all athletic endeavors, basic work is of the essence.

But in parallel, I started to explore other arts, a few years at a time, as opportunities and geography allowed. During my long Martial Arts career, I did practice assiduously: *Karatedo* of the *Wado-ryu*, *Shotokai* and *Kyokushinkai* schools, Full-contact *Karate*, *Taekwondo*, *Savate-Boxe Francaise* and two styles of *Ju-Jitsu*. Less intensively, I also did train in *Sankukai Karate*, *Capoeira*, *Krav Maga*, *Muay Thai* and some soft styles of *Kung-Fu*. This is how and where I developed my individual methods and own understanding of the Art of Kicking and also formed the basis from which to start my own personal research.

Sometime during this eclectic career, my travels took me to the *Shi-Heun* school of Sensei *Sidney Faige*. *Shi –Heun* is a *Shotokan*-based style mixed with *Judo* practice. The style emphasizes extreme conditioning, total fighting under various realistic rules sets and the personal quest for what works best for oneself. As this was only 1983, this was definitely

Sensei Sidney Faige with the winning Israeli National Karate team. Marc De Bremaeker and Roy Faige are on the right.

a precursor to the much later phenomena of Mixed Martial Arts. The fighting rules in the dojo were very close to today's UFC and relatives, but this did not hinder the success of the students in more traditional fighting tournaments, under milder rules. The hard training under all types of rules made it such that the direct disciples of *Sensei Faige* did roam the tournament scene undefeated for years.

Points tournament fighting was mainly WUKO (World Union of Karate Organizations) in these days. It generally boringly consisted in 2 competitors jumping up and down, waiting for the other to initiate a move, so as to be able to stop-reverse punch him. When my name was called for a fight in one of those point tournaments, there was spontaneous applause from the spectators, as they knew they were going to see, finally, some kicking. I apologize if this sounds like a boast, but the point I am trying to make and exemplify is that spectators and fans came for Martial Arts with *kicks*, not for an unrealistic form of boxing.

above: The authors fighting off the finals of a points-tournament in 1987

right: Marc De Bremaeker, in tournament, kicking

It is my strong belief that kicking is a big part of what made the Oriental Martial Arts so appealing. As I have already mentioned in articles and previous publications, I also do firmly argue that **kicking is more efficient than punching.** This usually makes many people stand up and disagree. This is a debate that has been going on for years, and I respectfully ask to be able to complete my sentence: I strongly believe that **kicking is more efficient than punching, <u>but proficiency takes much more time and work.</u>** When corrected this way, I hope my position will cause much less arguing. And I want to detail my position a bit.

Kicking is more efficient than punching:

... because of the longer range

... because the muscles of the leg are much more powerful than those of the arms

... because kicking targets, unlike punching, go from the toes up to the head

... because of the surprise effect: People still tend to expect less to be kicked than punched.

I readily admit that opponents of my position do have valid points. They will point out that kicks are inherently slower than punches, can be jammed because they only work at long ranges, and cannot be delivered from all positions. It is my experience that, *after a lot of dedicated work*, kicks can be as swift as punches, and can be used at all ranges and from all positions.

During all my training years, I invested a lot of time, personal drilling and research into Kicking Arts from all over the world. I tried all training tips gathered and I tried out all kicks variations in actual fights and tournaments. I so developed a personal kicking style based on my personal history. During this quest, I came across many treatises, but very few actually dedicated to kicking. The few works I found about kicking, although generally very good, were usually style-restricted, or unorganized. As I never found the kind of book I would have liked to have when I started my Martial Arts career, I decided to write it myself. There had never been an attempt, to the best of my knowledge, to compile and organize all the different kick types and variations, in order to offer a basis of personal exploration or to serve as a reference work for the kick-lover. I did try to start this, probably imperfectly, with my previous books *"The Essential Book of Martial Arts Kicks"* covering the essential *basic* kicks families and *"Low kicks"* studying the specifics of attacking the *Lower* Gate. I hope to continue this work with the present volume about the important **Stop Kicks**, and I pray that this work will be built upon by others. As I did underline that kicking proficiency requires a lot of drilling, I have also published a work about the basic drills that will help you reach the next level of proficiency. As in all athletic endeavors, it is the basic drills that will build the strong foundation needed and to which the really good athlete will come back to for further progress. *"Plyo-Flex Training for Explosive Martial Arts Kicks and other Performance Sports"* does present those basic but so-important exercises one should regularly practice for continuous improvement of kicking proficiency.

And last but certainly not least: It is important to underline that my strong views, do not in any way or form try to denigrate the punching arts. My philosophy is that Martial Arts are a whole with a world of different possible emphasis: A complete Martial Artist should be proficient in punching, kicking, throwing, grappling, evading, and more. But the Artist will have his own preferences and particular skills, of course. And now let me add the obvious: *There is no kicking without punching proficiency*! Punching is necessary for closing the gap, feinting, setting up a kick, following up, and more. This will be clear from most of the applications described in this work. And punching is sometimes the best or the only answer in some situations. I have known some extraordinary punching martial artists, using kicks only as feints and set-ups. On the other hand, great kickers, like *Bill "Superfoot" Wallace*, were extremely skilled punchers as well! (I remember well, in one of Bill's seminars, doing more push-ups in an hour than in the whole previous month). Punch and Kick: well-rounded is the secret!

This leads me naturally to another obvious point: I would not want my views to be misunderstood as an appeal to always kick when fighting, and especially not to always *high-kick*. Not only is it not suitable for all morphologies and mind sets, but even the best kicker in the world should **not** deliver a high kick **just because he can**! A kick or a high kick should be delivered only *when* and *because* it is suitable for the specific situation the fighter is currently in. Obvious, maybe, but worth reminding! In someone else's words:

Take things as they are. Punch when you have to punch. Kick when you have to kick.
~ Bruce Lee

Series Introduction

This book is not a "How to" book for the beginner, but, hopefully, a reference work for the experienced Martial Artist. It presupposes the knowledge of stances, footwork, and concepts of centerline, guards, distance, evasions and more. It also expects from the reader a good technical level in his chosen Martial style, including kicking. As this work is building upon the *Essential* basic level towards more sophisticated kicking maneuvers, all *Essential Kicks* are considered mastered from the author's point of view. The reader is invited to consult previous work already mentioned above. This book is intended as a tool for self-exploration and research about kicking outside experienced Artists' specific style. Therefore, the description of the different kicks is very short and typical examples are only briefly explained. The author relies more on photos and illustrations to exemplify his point. Let the reader try it and adapt it to his liking and morphology.

The author tends to prefer drawings over photographs to be able to underline salient points sometimes hidden in photos.

The experienced trainee will probably notice quickly that the basic background of the author is Japanese *Karate*. This cannot be avoided but was not deliberate. This book aspires to be as "style-less" as possible, as its purpose is to bridge across the different schools on the basis of common immutable principles. The author's philosophy is that Martial Arts are an interconnected whole, where styles are just interpretations of some principles and their adaptation to certain sets of strategies, rules, cultural constraints, or morphologies. It is one and same thing, although it may seem different from different angles. In the pictures and illustrations, the reader can see technical differences and adaptations from different styles. This is done on purpose to underscore the style-less philosophy of the treatise. Sometimes the foot of the standing leg is flat on the floor, as required in traditional Japanese styles, and sometimes the heel is up as in certain deliveries of Korean arts. It should be clear that the biomechanical principles are identical for trained artists and the small differences of emphasis are meaningless. It is more important for a trainee to adapt the technique to his morphology and preferences, once it is well mastered. This book definitely does not pretend to present an axiomatic way to kick! In the same vein, arms during kicking are sometimes close to the body in hermetic guard and sometimes loose and counterbalancing the kicking move. Hands can be open, or fists tight.

Like in previous efforts, it has proved very difficult to name and organize the kicks into and within groups. The author has given the techniques descriptive names in English, whenever possible commonly used names. But the more complex, exotic and hybrid kicks have sometimes either several different appellations in use or none, while being difficult to describe. The names the author has chosen could certainly be disputed and improved upon by some. For the most basic kicks common to all styles, we have added the respective original foreign names. The author apologizes in advance to the purists of all styles: It is clear that the description of a technique cannot be in all details valid for all styles (For example, the basic front kick is taught differently in Shotokan karate than in TaeKwonDo. The original foreign names in Japanese, Korean, Chinese or Portuguese are just there as an indication for further research by the reader. It should also be noted that some techniques have different names in different schools of the same art! For the more complex or exotic kicks, we have purposely omitted original names. Only when a kick is especially typical of a certain style, did we mention it, as a tribute to the specific school. The author also apologizes for his arbitrary transcription of foreign names, as purists could dispute the way it was done.

The kicks presented in this volume are tagged "Advanced". This does not necessarily mean that they are more difficult to execute than the Essential basic kicks. On the contrary. Besides being a requisite of some form of classification, it mainly means that the principles behind the "basic" kicks should be first thoroughly mastered. A Front Stop Kick is relatively easy to perform and slightly different than a regular Front Kick. But for maximum power, it is important to follow the same principles of a basic Front Kick, with chambering, kicking through and chamber back. And the principles of the leg development stay the same for the more difficult Flying Front Kick. And even if a Low Front kick seems easy to perform, it will be done so under the same principles already mastered for maximum speed and power. Once the principles behind the basic Front Kick are mastered, all other "Advanced" kicks will be faster and more powerful. *This is all about mastering the basics and principles first*, and only later trying out variations in all kinds of situations, fancier or not. This is, by the way, true for any other physical activity. But because Advanced Kicks are more a variation on the theme of their underlying basic kicks, they will be presented in all their complexity by many variations in specific applications.

This volume will not detail Essential basic kicks. If needed for the clarity of the narrative, some of them will be very briefly illustrated as a reminder. This volume deals with **Stop Kicks** only, as a variation of all six basic categories of Essential Kicks presented in previous work (Front, Side, Back, Roundhouse, Hook and Crescent Kicks). Further volumes are in preparation to present the spectacular Flying kicks, the situational Ground kicks, the complex Multiple kicks, the sneaky Feint kicks, the surprising Suicide kicks and the devastating Joint kicks.

Some Advanced Kicks have been omitted, as the author felt he had to draw the line somewhere. Again the decision was arbitrary, and could be considered as open for discussion. First have been omitted the whole range of nuances of a given kicks: As already mentioned, the same basic kicks are delivered in slightly different ways in all different styles and schools. The small differences come from the different emphasis of each style, and do not alter the basic principles. The author therefore described the kicks in the way his own experience dictates as best, and each reader can adapt it to his own personality. Many possible variations are presented for completeness in the applications though.

Secondly, hybrid kicks variations have been omitted, as the infinite number of intermediate possible deliveries in between two kicks would make this endeavor ridiculous. For example, many possible kicks as hybrids of Front and Roundhouse Kicks exist, each one with different levels of emphasis on the "front" side and the "roundhouse" side.

Kicks combinations, and kick-punch combinations are infinite in numbers and will not be presented. Knee strikes, although very effective and versatile, will not be presented; for the purpose of this work, they will not be considered as kicks.

Knee Strike

The remaining Stop Kicks, which will be presented in this work, will be so, generally, in a set descriptive way: After a brief <u>general</u> introduction and the <u>description</u> of the kick (mainly by illustrations), the main <u>key points</u> to remember for a good execution will be noted. Please remember that the book is intended for conversant martial artists. The relevant <u>targets</u> to be kicked in most applications will be mentioned, although only general targets will be mentioned: The specific and precise vulnerable points are out of the scope of this volume. Examples of <u>typical application</u> will then be detailed and illustrated. The typical application will generally be, unless irrelevant, a detailed use or set up of the given kick in a tournament-type situation. This will generally be a movements combination based on alternating different attack angles or/and levels (For example: hi-lo-hi, or/and outside/inside/outside), or the Progressive Indirect Attack principle as it is called by *Jeet Kune Do* artists. The tactical principle involved will not be detailed or presented systematically though, as it is beyond the scope of this volume. Of course, those applications will also usually be relevant to real life situation, and training work. Whenever possible, <u>specific training</u> tips to improve the given kick will be detailed. The specific training section will be brief and will only deal with the very specific characteristics of the kick and the ways to perfect them; general kick training guidelines are outside the scope of this book. The training of a Stop Kick is generally also the drilling of the corresponding Essential basic kick. Last, and in order to widen the scope of applications, an additional example of the use of the kick will be presented, generally more suitable to a <u>self-defense</u> or <u>mixed martial arts</u> application.

And now, let us go to STOP KICKS...

I question myself every day. That's what I still find motivating about this. I don't have the answers, I don't pretend that I do just because I won the match. Just keep fighting and maybe something good happens.
~ Andre Agassi

Introduction to Stop Kicks

"There are three kinds of fighters: the aggressive fighter who charges in blindly trying to get the upper hand, the defensive fighter who blocks and evades until his opponent is tired, and then the most dangerous type of fighter, the one who waits for his opponent to make a mistake."
~ Aaron B. Powell

Front Pushing Kick in free fighting –
Marc De Bremaeker

A good offense is the best defense

Stop kicks are by all standards the highest form of kicking and the most sophisticated way of fighting. In some of its forms, it is the embodiment of the Japanese ***Sen-no-sen*** principle: preempt an attack before it takes form. Ideally, you should kick, just as the opponent decides upon his own attack launch. Although to an outside observer it seems as you are the attacker, you preempt a real attack: It is both a highly moral and extremely effective defense.

In all its forms, stop-kicking is the most effective way to kick for many reasons: for starters, it adds the energy of the forward momentum of your opponent to the power of your own kick. It is also psychologically very frustrating and damaging to him: on top of the direct damage, it will make your opponent wary of further attacks. And the Stop Kick catches an opponent as he is most unprepared: he is already committed to his attack, he is in the process of opening himself and he is at his least ready for a block or an evasion. As you attack him yourself, you also befuddle his range calculations: he was counting on you staying in place or retreating, and here you come!

But stop kicking is a difficult skill to acquire and master; it requires drilling for speed and for explosive delivery, gaining mastery of footwork, and investing in a lot of intelligent sparring to learn to "read" an opponent's intentions.

Some well-known and effective styles rely a lot on stop-kicking and obstruction-kicking as a matter of tactics or even strategy. *Wing-Chun* artists will easily foil kicking or even striking attacks with their low stop-kicks. *Jeet Kune Do* kick defense is highly reliant on obstruction; and their version of the low kicks are much drilled as stop-kicks, interestingly <u>with virtually no</u> <u>chambering</u>. *Savate's Coup de pied bas* will stop many kicks in their first stages of development, as a matter of daily training.

Early observers of the MMA's meteoric rise will remember the great *Royce Gracie's* first appearances against cocky but fierce kickboxing fighters: he used to stop-kick and obstruct their kicks until the right moment of his shooting for their legs; of course, once on the ground, he owned them…

Stop-kicking, attrition kicking and obstruction kicking are obviously under-drilled and under-appreciated; they are a great secret weapon to develop for the well-rounded Martial Artist's arsenal.

Many Low Kicks, as presented in our previous book in the series, are in fact mostly used as stop-kicks or obstruction maneuvers. The reader is invited to refer to *Low Kicks* (Turtle Press) for many more examples and applications of highly effective Stop Kicks.

He who is prudent and lies in wait for an enemy who is not, will be victorious.
~ Sun Tzu

Stop Kick Types

Stop Kicks can be delivered "lightly" by simply placing your foot in the path of a developing kick or step. Stop Kicks can be delivered "lightly" to an immobile front leg as a precaution when closing the distance with an opponent. These are still Stop Kicks, and very effective ones, but they will not be described as such; they simply are faster but less powerful versions of the full-powered Stop Kicks we shall study. One should only remember that all intermediate versions between a no-chamber light obstruction tap and a full-power, momentum-stopping, crushing kick are valid and relevant.

Full Stop Kicks can be categorized in 4 broad types:

(1) Kicking the attacking limb. You kick the incoming arm or leg to block it, while inflicting pain and damage. You can either kick into the path of the attack to stop the forward movement, or kick it sideways to inflect its course. These are not fully stop-kicks, as they do not ensure full stopping of the attacker's forward momentum. They are more "leg blocks" than Stop Kicks, but will generally be effective enough to at least dissipate the energy of the attack. Of course, like always, there is a whole array of nuances in between the two and classification can be difficult; we shall present many examples in the text. For the sake of completeness, we will present succinctly the array of possible *Leg Blocks* in this introduction. This category is illustrated below.

Crescent kick to thigh of developing Roundhouse Kick

(2) Kicking straight to the incoming body or legs. This is the intrinsic Stop Kick as its name describes it. Your attacker lunges forward to hit you, and you stop him by kicking forward into his body or his legs. You kick into his forward momentum to stop him, aiming at impaling him on to your kick. This is based on speed and being able to read your opponent's intentions while hiding yours: your opponent calculates his move on the assumption you will be retreating or staying in place and you foil his

plans by going *forward* into his attack. It may seem dangerous, but in fact is probably the safest of tactics: Even if his attack is surprising by its speed, angle and power, it will not be at the apex of its energy when in mid-flight! You, on the other end, are calculating your move to be at full kick development at mid-distance. This is even a more logical course of action against a circular attack: While your opponent's attack comes around, you take the shortest and fastest route of the straight centerline. The illustration below shows the cleanest of examples: the stop straight Front Kick against a developing (circular) Roundhouse Kick.

Rear-leg penetrating front kick travels faster than a circular rear-leg roundhouse kick

(3) Kicking the incoming attacker around the straight line. This is the opposite of the example presented above. It can just be any kick, although preferably to a sensitive target like the head or groin, as the basic idea here is "beating him to the punch" as the expression goes. It is a 'timing' kick, aiming at catching the opponent at his most vulnerable moment: just as he starts to attack. *As you are not physically stopping his forward momentum,* you have to score at a sensitive target in order to make him stop. This requires experience and a lot of training, but is extremely effective. Even if not perfect, the timing stop-kick will always foil the full development of his attack while putting him physically and mentally off-balance. There is a need for some experience in tell-tales'-reading for those "timing" kicks; it may seem sometimes as a "Sixth Sense", but is merely intuitive experience built on practice. Straightforward examples are presented on the opposite page.

Hopping Roundhouse Stop Kick during the chambering of a stick attack

A more complex way to deliver this particular type of Stop Kick is by using *angling* kicks after, or while, evading the centerline. Some <u>Essential</u> Angling Kicks have been presented in our first book to which the reader is invited to refer; among them: The Oblique Front Kick, the Phantom Groin Kick, the Oblique Back Side Kick, the Oblique Roundhouse Kick, the Downward Back Kick, the Oblique Hook Kick, the Half-pivot Hook Kick and the Oblique Spin-back Hook Kick. A few relevant examples are illustrated below.

In-place front-leg Hook Stop Kick, timing a reverse punch

The Essential Oblique Roundhouse Kick, angling out of the trajectory of a rear-leg penetrating Front Kick

The Essential Oblique Spin-back Hook Kick, angling out of the trajectory of a rear-leg penetrating Front Kick

Rolling-in Spin-back Hook Kick against a rear-leg full Roundhouse Kick

Half-pivot Hook Kick, angling out of the trajectory of a full-step lunge punch

(4) Kicking before the attack can start. ("**Attack on preparation**"). This is the highest level of stop-kicking, the one every Martial Artist should strive for: your opponent has decided to attack and basically has ordered his body to launch; you feel it and preempt it from even starting. To an outside observer, it may look like you are the aggressor. And any kick is relevant for this type of stop-kicking. It may read far-fetched, but every experienced Martial Artist knows how years of training hone the instincts and the ability to unconsciously "read" the opponent. This is the famous *Sen no sen* principle of the Japanese Martial Arts, touted, for example, by the famous swordsman *Miyamoto Musashi*. The Japanese high-level Artists even discern three different stages in the fraction of a second needed for a preemptive attack: *"Sakki"* (The ability to feel the decision of attack as it forms), *"Sen-no-sen"* (The decision of preempting the attack), and *"Senken"* (The start of the execution).

Stop Kick on preparation; it may seem as if you are the assailant

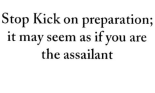

More Stop-kick types

Some schools also include into *Stop-kicking* two other types of stopping techniques:

__Attack on completion__: Kicking to catch the opponent at full extension of his attack: this requires mastery of footwork and distance. You move the target—your head or body—away from the incoming attacking limb; if possible, move just a few inches. And you develop your own attack so as to catch the opponent as he reaches full extension of his attack. The retreat or evasion must be gradual and in tandem with the attack, in a way that unconsciously lets the opponent believe that he is going to connect (The '*Aiki*' spirit and principle). This kind of kick can be devastating, as an overextended opponent opens all his vital areas to the Stop Kick or Counter Kick. See examples below.

Evade the Side Kick by pulling back your midsection and groin-kick him at his full extension

Evade the Low Kick to counter with an Essential Downward Heel Kick as the opponent is still pulled by his momentum

Attack on recovery: Kicking to catch the opponent as he swings back into original position after an unsuccessful attack. You evade just as in the previous type, and then attack as he retreats back to his original fighting stance.

Low Kick on recovery from a Roundhouse Kick attack

Front Kick on recovery from a rear-leg Penetrating Front Kick

Those tactics are extremely useful and efficient, and we shall scatter a few examples throughout the text. But they will be discussed in detail only in further books about strategy; we will not consider them here as *Stop Kicks* per se in this book.

An important other distinction to make, at least in the tactical sense, is the following: <u>All stop kicks can be used in</u> an *offensive* <u>manner by drawing the attacker into a specific attack.</u> This is valid for all real Stop Kick-types. This is the principle of "**Attack by Drawing**": You open your guard or place yourself in such a way, that the opponent will see an opening beckoning him for a (more or less) specific attack. As soon as you feel his attack taking form, you will stop-kick him. This is more of a *tactical* distinction to be discussed in a further volume, but it would differentiate between "real" defensive Stop Kicks and offensive "drawing" Stop Kicks. Examples of this luring your opponent in will be given throughout the text as well.

The opportunity to secure ourselves
against defeat lies in our own hands, but
the opportunity of defeating the enemy is
provided by the enemy himself.
~ Sun Tzu

Stop-Kicking Variations of Regular Kicks

As already repeatedly mentioned, all kicks can be Stop Kicks. The serious Martial Artist will make his up own mind about what to use in a specific situation, and which kicks are more suited to his personality and physiology.

Some variations of the basic Essential Kicks are, though, intrinsically more suited to stop-kicking:

1. *Angled Kicks*, as mentioned earlier. Kicking while or after evading the line of attack by side-stepping. It could be argued that Drop Kicks and Flying Kicks are a vertical evasion from the line of attack, and therefore, in the same category.

Oblique Spin-back Hook Kick.: Get out of the line of attack and deliver the Hook Kick into his forward momentum

2. *Switch Kicks*. Switching legs more or less in place, to allow for rear-leg kicking and therefore more power to stop an opponent in his tracks.

Switch Front Kick: Switch legs while adjusting distance, then execute a rear-leg Front Kick into the Spin-back attack

3. *Body-bent Kicks*. Getting the target (Head & Upper body) away from the attack while kicking.

Hand-on-floor Side Kick: Side-stop-kick a stick attack, place hand on floor to remove the upper body from the danger zone

Those Essential Kicks have already been presented in detail in our previous book, but an example of each is presented in this chapter to place them into perspective from the Stop Kick-point of view.

Leg Blocks

As mentioned, and for the sake of completeness, we will present succinctly the different types of Leg Blocks available to the Martial Artist. Some can be considered Stop Kicks or near-Stop Kicks, other are simply blocks that need to be followed by a counter. Many are also simple obstruction techniques, not very powerful but extremely unsettling and with the potential of giving you openings for subsequent maneuvers. Leg Blocks may seem to some futile and unrealistic exercises; that is far from the truth. But like every other technique, they have to be used judiciously and only when suitable. They generally will only be applicable when the opponent over-commits himself; for example, after you have made him believe that you always retreat a lot as soon as he attacks. And think for a second about the impact of a kick to the shin of a leg that is powerfully travelling towards it; or the damage a full-powered Crescent Kick will do when connecting with an extended elbow!

Example of Leg Block: Inside front-leg Block of a low Roundhouse Kick

Inside front-leg Block *(Uchi Ashibo kake uke – Karatedo)*, against a Front Kick in this example

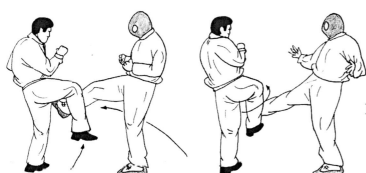

Inside front-leg block of a Front Kick

Application of *Uchi Ashibo Kake Uke*

<u>Outside front-leg Block</u> *(Soto Ashibo kake uke – Karatedo)*, against a Roundhouse for example

Outside front-leg block of low Straight-leg Roundhouse

<u>Outside rear-leg Block</u>, against a low Roundhouse for example

Outside rear-leg block against Low Kick

<u>Front Kick Block</u>, against a Front Kick for example

Front Kick push-block against a chambering Front Kick

<u>Upward Front Kick Block</u>, against a punch for example

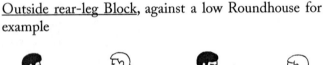

Front-leg Upward Front Kick block against a full-step lunge punch

<u>Side Kick Block</u> *(Sokuto Osae Uke – Karatedo)*, against a Front Kick for example

Front-leg Side Kick Block of Front Kick

<u>Upward Side Kick Block</u>, against a punch for example

Front-leg Upward Side Kick block against jab

Soccer Front Kick Block *(Sokutei Osae uke – Karatedo)*, against a Front Kick for example

**Soccer low Front Kick Block
against a chambering Front Kick**

Inside Crescent Kick Block *(Mikazuki Geri Uke – Karatedo)*, against a punch for example

**Full power rear-leg Crescent Kick
against incoming arm of lunging jab**

Outside Crescent Kick Block *(Gyacku Mikazuki Geri Uke - Karatedo)*, against a Front Kick for example

**Rear-leg Outside Crescent Kick to
the knee of a chambering Front Kick**

Downward Heel Kick Block *(Kakato Geri Uke - Karatedo)*, against a Spin-back Hook Kick for example

**Rear-leg "Axe" Kick to the incoming leg of a
Spin-back Hook Kick; potentially
joint-damaging**

Training for Stop Kicks

Training for Stop Kicks is much more than just drilling the kicks and the combinations presented, although it starts there.

First, the reader is invited to try to execute the kicks presented in the spirit in which they are presented. The reader is supposed to be a practicing Martial Artist and will have no problem executing the techniques presented, as they are slight variations of regular basic techniques. In fact, sometimes, it is only the mindset that differentiates the kick from the corresponding basic kick.

The reader should then try to drill the applications presented, both in the *Applications* and in the *Self-defense* sections. Some of those combinations may seem far-fetched or inappropriate to some readers, because it does not align with their style, because the way free-fighting is regulated in their art/sport or because they do not "believe" in it. The author begs you to drill these applications anyway: the body should be subjected to all possible situations and ways to fight, even if the specific technique would not be used willfully by the trainee. Just like mental intuition is in fact based on a long experience at the subconscious level, real fighting is done automatically by your body and your *unconscious* mind, based on all the experience gathered in training. You never know when your body will decide in the fight that a certain "new" reaction is the right thing to do. You can plan a general tactic before a fight, but once in the fire of the action, it is your unconscious that will react: if you would have to think about a reaction to a strike, you would be in serious trouble. Therefore you must feed "data" to your body and mind, by drilling time and again all sorts of combination, techniques, reactions, positioning, and more.

I can illustrate this with a personal anecdote:

What would become my favorite stop-kicking technique—the 'timing' Hook Stop Kick—just appeared suddenly of its own volition in my free-fighting practice. I had drilled it in training, but along with many other Stop Kicks, and I had not felt any special affinity for it before. In fact, I used to Roundhouse stop-kick my opponents most of the time beforehand. My body and mind did probably identify this particular kick as most suitable to my morphology and personality, and un-holstered it at the right moment in a no-thinking situation. Needless to say that, from then on, I did give it particular attention and further training. It became my most natural and potent competing weapon. The point

is: Try everything and drill it hard; your body and mind will do the rest.

And try not to judge other styles and other ways of fighting, you can never really know. Not everything in your style or not everything working for you is necessarily the best for others. Among the comments I received after the publication of "*The Essential Book of Martial Arts Kicks*", was from a reader that did not agree to the use of a Drop Kick presented as an application against a mugger in the *Self-Defense* section. Why go to the ground against a mugger? Although I personally would not use this particular technique, it is certainly valid if used by some artists like Capoeira practitioners, MMA ground fighters, some Indonesian stylists and many more. You could find yourself on the ground by accident too! I have had the greatest difficulty in handling ground fighters myself, and I would not be quick to judge any technique. I advise the reader to keep things in perspective, to be respectful of the emphasis of other styles and to try everything. And to keep an open mind…

Once you have tried and mastered the kicks and applications presented and have worked on the training tips, you still are very far from being a stop-kicker!

Stop Kicking being a mindset, you should in fact work on completely different things. To be a good stop-kicker you must work very hard on the following:

1. *Partner reading.* You have to develop your intuition (= experience) of when your opponent starts his attack. You have to learn to read all tell-tales of an imminent attack. You have to start discerning instinctively which type of attack is coming. There is no substitute to free-fighting, in the widest possible set of rules. There is no way to teach, and probably to really explain in words, how to do that. Concentrate on partner reading during part of your free-fighting routines and slowly build your abilities. This is the *Sen No Sen* of Japanese Martial Arts, but it exists in all other Arts and sports. It must be built gradually, because it takes place in the subconscious mind.

2. *No telegraph.* You should aim at "reading" your opponent and, at the same time, make sure he cannot "read" you. This is always true in free-fighting, but it is even more important if you are working on stop-kicking skills. This is easier to improve, as you can execute your techniques in front of a mirror, while trying to explode into the kick without *any* preceding movement or mimic. You can have your partner checking you for telltales in training and in free-

fighting. Check yourself for the telltales you find in others; maybe you are making the same natural mistake. Maybe your "weightless" front foot ready for a 'timing' front-leg kick is obvious, just like that of your partner? You will have to work on concealing the fact that most of your body weight is on the rear leg; it's relatively easy but you need to get used to it... Remember: it will not help you much to be a good reader of intentions if you, yourself, are an open book to others.

3. _Speed_. Stop-kicking is about beating your opponent to the punch, literally and pun intended. There will be no such thing if you are not fast. Speed of reaction is partially covered in the preceding points (Reading the partner …and reacting) and the following (Reacting with focus) points. Left to discuss is the important part of the _speedy_ delivery of the kick. That will come with intensive drilling of the basic kicks and the building of confidence. To be fast, a kick must be delivered with relaxed muscles until the moment of impact. This is the way kicks must be drilled until they become second nature. Further training should include a **combination** of plyometric exercises and intense stretching, so as to retain the necessary qualities leading to fast kicking (Explosiveness and Flexibility). The reader is invited to consult our book on the subject (_Plyo Flex_ – Turtle Press).

4. _Focus_. Stop Kicking requires what is called _Zanshin_ in Japanese: focus, concentration, single-purpose attitude. Once you stop-kick, you must be fully committed and explode forward. There cannot be a second thought as it would impede speed and mental domination of the opponent. Going forward into an attack requires a special mindset. Focus must be a conscious part of your training, whether in training or in free-fighting.

Those "intangibles" are the most important tenets of Stop-kicking. The techniques that we shall present are the basis only. The basis is necessary, but not enough; it is only the beginning of the journey.

Recommended reading about all those tenets of training for stop-kicking, or stop-punching for all that matters, is the excellent book: _Timing in the Fighting Arts_ by L. Christensen and W. Demeere (Turtle Press)

Chapter presentation

As is now clear, all kicks can be used as Stop Kicks. They are just kicks used in specific situations, but are not basically different from the original basic kick. This is why only the most typical of stop-kicks will be presented here, and in a more succinct manner than for previous books. The Stop Kick is in itself a '_Typical Application_' of the basic Essential kick presented in other volumes of this book series. Therefore, many references will be made to other kicks previously presented and the examples will be kept to a minimum. The skilled reader already understands that, for example, all Oblique Kicks evading the centerline, and all "Cutting" Kicks of our previous "_Low Kicks_" book, are—in fact—Stop Kicks. Any "timing" Kick, delivered as the opponent only decides to launch his own attack, is also a Stop Kick.

Not high quality photo but a classic 'timing' Hook Stop Kick in combat by Marc De Bremaeker

"There may be people that have more talent than you, but there is no excuse for anyone to work harder than you do."

~Derek Jeter

Stop Kicks are common-place in redoubtable Muay Thai: *Teep Trong* by Aviva Giveoni

Forward pushing Stop Kick to incoming opponent

Front Kick Push-Block against Front Kick chamber

Front Kick Push-Block against Spin-back Hook Kick

Mikazuki Geri Uke – Crescent Kick Block

The slightly different trajectory of the stop-version of the Side Kick

1. The Front Pushing Kick and other Front Stop Kicks

Ahp Cha Meelgi (Tae Kwon Do), Teep Trong (Muay Thai), Teep Kick (Common name), Jeet Tek (Wing Chung Kung Fu), Sokugyacku Geri (Nin Jitsu)

General

Pushing Kicks are different from their relevant parent kicks: They are less powerful and delivered differently. True to their name, they are more pushes than kicks, and they are mainly used to keep the opponent away at a distance. They can still be effective as kicks though, especially when well-timed to take advantage of the opponent's forward momentum.

The Front Pushing Kick is very much in use in the very effective and realistic hard sport of *Muay Thai*, which proves how important this kick is for real practice. If you are not a very good grappler or good in-fighter, it is important to be able to keep the adversary at the distance that is comfortable to you; this kick is a great tool to do just that. It is also a great kick to push the opponent away to the perfect range for your following kick, a rear leg full-powered kick for example.

The less known traditional parent Martial Art of Thai Boxing—*Muay Thai Boran*—has a series of set techniques to be drilled by the student and called *Mae Mai Muay Thai*, in the spirit of '*Ippon Kumite*' or '*Katas*' of the Japanese Arts. One of these set drills is called *Mon Yan*

Lak (Pillar Support) and is a Front-leg Front Pushing Stop Kick against a reverse punching attack. Another technique of the series, called *Viroon Hok Glab* (Bird Jump), is a (slightly crescent) rear-leg Front Pushing Stop Kick to the hip of a Roundhouse-kicking opponent.

It is interesting to note that the devastating *Nin-Jitsu* version of this kick is delivered with the foot tilted outwards, to allow connecting with the heel and targeting the hip joint with precision.

Muay Thai's *Teep Trong*

Traditional Mae Mai Muay Thai's *Mon Yan Lak*

Traditional Mae Mai Muay Thai's *Viroon Hok Glab*

Description

The delivery of this pushing kick is different from the delivery of the regular Essential Penetrating Front Kick. It is faster, it is earlier on its final trajectory, but it is less powerful; that is the trade-in. Basically the chamber of the kick is at mid-trajectory, so as to place the weapon (ball-of-foot, plant-of-foot or heel) directly between you and your opponent as fast as possible: the figure below shows clearly the difference in chambering position. Because of the relatively smaller distance from chamber position to target, the kick has a "pushy" feel to it and is therefore less powerful. But it should be drilled and delivered as a *kick* first and foremost, and not as a push: thrust your hips forcefully into the kick. The push will be a real but secondary benefit.

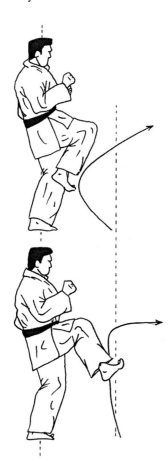

Comparative chamber position for a regular front-leg Front Kick and a front-leg Pushing Front Stop Kick

Because of its use as a Stop Kick, it is usually delivered with the front leg: it is faster and it is the closest weapon to the opponent. But rear-leg kicking is appropriate in many circumstances and the delivery will be from the same chamber described above. The photo below shows the delivery of a rear-leg Front Pushing Stop Kick. And always remember also that the kick can be delivered as a *Switch Kick* to accommodate distance for the rear-leg delivery if so you wish. The illustrations below give an example of a rear-leg version of the kick against a cross punch; remember that the *pushing* will probably further distance your opponent and that you could have to execute a step after landing in order to catch up with him for your follow-up techniques.

Rear-leg Front Pushing Stop kick

Key points

- Get forcefully and dynamically into chamber position. And no stopping there: this is a smooth uninterrupted move.

- Thrust the hips into the kick (See below), just like for any Front Kick.

- Time the kick to make use of the forward surge of your opponent's attack: ideal contact point is just before his mid-delivery.

Hip thrust into the Pushing Front Stop Kick

Rear-leg Front Pushing Stop Kick against reverse punch; follow up with stepping Reverse Punch

Targets

This kick is a straight line Stop Kick; it is therefore supposed to stop a fully powered forward attack by your opponent. Preferred targets are center and mid-body, close to his center of gravity: solar plexus, lower belly and hip level.

Attacking the legs is also a good momentum-stopper but it needs more accuracy: target the hip joints all the way down to the knee, (See Photo and Illustrations below). A Front Pushing Stop Kick just above the knee will not only stop the opponent in his tracks but also become an efficient joint-damaging Low Kick (*High-chamber Low Stomp Front Kick*; see our previous book '*Low Kicks*' from Turtle Press). In the example below, a jab in opposite stances is stopped by such a kick and followed by a rear-leg Roundhouse Kick.

Pushing Front Kick to the opponent's front knee

Front-leg Front Pushing Stop Kick with some stomping to the knee

Typical application

The series below shows a body-stop application, with a front-leg *Teep Kick* stopping the delivery of a 'Low Kick' (Straight-leg Roundhouse Kick, *Te Tut* in *Muay Thai*).

Front-leg Pushing Front Stop Kick against a developing rear-leg Roundhouse

The series below shows a body-stop application, with a front-leg Pushing Front Kick, against a rear-leg classic Front Kick.

Front-leg Pushing Front Kick is faster than rear-leg full-chamber Front Kick

The follow series shows a rear-leg Front Pushing Kick to the body of an opponent trying a rear-leg Roundhouse.

Straight rear-leg Front Kick should be faster than a circular rear-leg Roundhouse

Kicks to the *joints* of an attacking opponent are definite stopping moves, especially to the hip joint close to the center of gravity. The figures below show a first joint attack that will disturb the delivery of a reverse punch: A front-leg Pushing Front Kick to the hip joint/high front thigh of the opponent, as soon as you feel the attack taking form. Follow up by controlling his shoulder to get on his blind side and knee him in the body. You can finish him off, as in this example, with a Downward Heel Kick to his exposed neck.

Front-leg Pushing Front Stop Kick to the hip joint of the attacking opponent

The series below shows another Joint Kick application: You front-leg stop-kick his hip joint (close to gravity center) as he develops a rear-leg Roundhouse. Catch up with him as he falls back, for example with a Spin-back Back Kick.

Another application of the front-leg Pushing Front Stop Kick to the hip joint

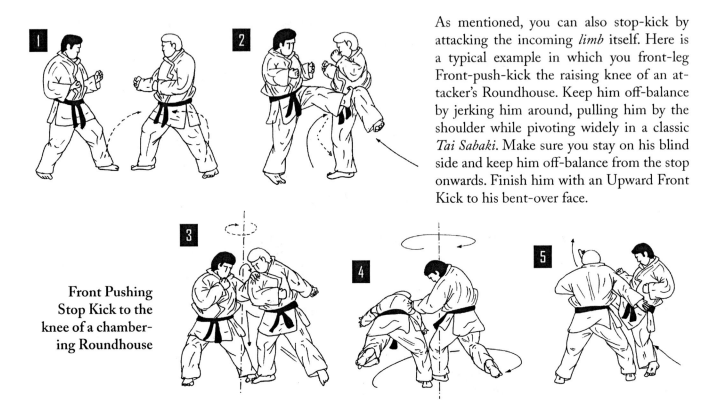

As mentioned, you can also stop-kick by attacking the incoming *limb* itself. Here is a typical example in which you front-leg Front-push-kick the raising knee of an attacker's Roundhouse. Keep him off-balance by jerking him around, pulling him by the shoulder while pivoting widely in a classic *Tai Sabaki*. Make sure you stay on his blind side and keep him off-balance from the stop onwards. Finish him with an Upward Front Kick to his bent-over face.

Front Pushing Stop Kick to the knee of a chambering Roundhouse

The illustrations below show the same kind of stop-kick against the raising knee of a *Front* Kick. The follow-up presented is interesting: Switch legs airborne for a fast Upward Front Kick to his exposed groin.

Pushing Stop Kick to the knee of a chambering Front Kick, and a punishing follow-up

As mentioned in the introduction, the key to successful stop-kicking is the mastery of *distance*. Footwork and switch-kicking are sometimes needed. The series spanning the bottom of these pages shows a Front Stop Kick *after a half-step retreat for distance-adjusting*: As your opponent initiates a reverse punch, you pull back the front leg—halfway—and deliver the Stop Kick with the (formerly) rear leg. Angle out when landing to get out of the centerline, and jab. Follow up, for example with a body Roundhouse and/or a sweep.

Specific training

- It is critical to drill this kick with a partner executing real attacks that you will have to stop. There is no alternative to free-fighting.

- Train against a bag swung towards you by a partner (See Illustration at right): drill front-leg kicks, rear-leg kicks and switching-legs kicks. Train at different ranges from the bag position. Your partner should let the bag go naturally at the beginning, but later, as you become proficient, he should *throw* the bag at you so that you can perfect your stopping power.

Stop-kicking can only be mastered by free-fighting

Drill stop-kicks on a heavy bag swung at you by a partner

Half-a-step back will give perfect range for a rear-leg Stop Kick against a reverse punch

Self-defense

All examples presented above were also relevant to self-defense or MMA fighting; the following examples are even more so. This kick is a great Stop Kick against "Low kicks" (low Straight-leg Roundhouses) too: the figures below show how to stop-kick your assailant's raising knee with your front foot, in an opposite-stances set-up. Follow-up with your own 'Low Kick' (Straight-leg Roundhouse to his legs).

Stop-kick the knee of a classic Low kick

The illustrations below show, again, the classic use of the Front Pushing Stop Kick against all forms of Spin-back Kicks. But this time, the follow-up will be more devastating. Kick the hips or bottom of your assailant as he spins back. Keep going after his back as he is thrown off-balance: In this example a hopping Side Stomp Kick is presented; but it also could be a Front Kick or a Side Kick to the kidney, among many other possibilities.

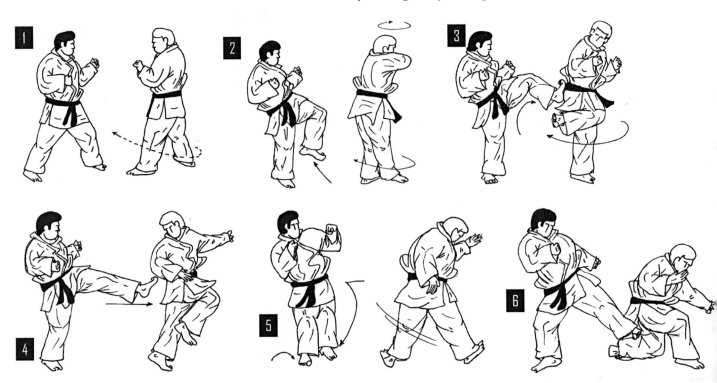

In a self-defense situation, you can attack your "pushed" assailant's offered back or offered back knee if warranted

In a self-defense situation, the classic Pushing Front Stop Kick against a developing rear-leg Roundhouse—described several times in this section—should aim at the *groin* rather than at the hip joint or incoming leg. This is illustrated below, with an aggressive follow-up, capped by a classic Essential Upward Hook Back Kick.

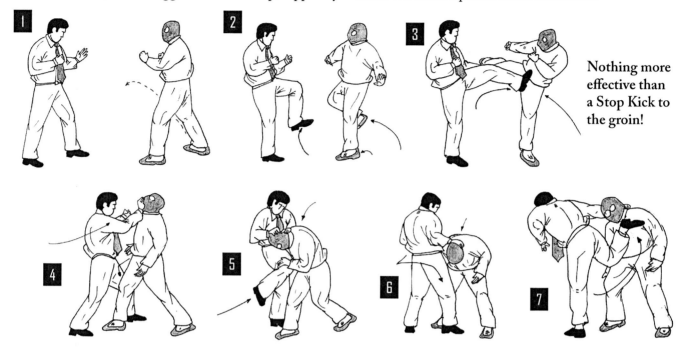

Nothing more effective than a Stop Kick to the groin!

The great thing about Stop Kicks is that they catch your opponent totally off-balance as he is concentrating on his own intended or developing attack. If well executed, this will allow you to follow-up easily with your own techniques on a befuddled opponent. The photos below show how a Pushing Front Stop Kick at the very start of an attack will allow you to go for a twin tackle, if you are a good ground-fighter.

Stop-kick at the very start of the opponent's move and shoot for his legs

Classic *Muay Thai*—and therefore inherently efficient—is the stop-kicking of the early stages of a "Low Kick" in order to deliver a deep and fully-hipped circular Elbow Strike. Drill this very hard combination, as illustrated below, and feel free to keep striking.

A *Muay Thai* combo against a developing Straight-leg Roundhouse: *Teep* Kick and *Soak Kang* (Elbow Strike)

Illustrative Photos

The Pushing Front Kick looks very typical at impact

Stop-kicking the knee of a chambering Front Kick

The classic Essential Penetrating Front Kick; no pushing there!

Most Essential Front Kick variations can be used as Stop Kicks, such as: (a) Heel Front Kick, (b)Tilted-heel Front Kick and (c) Foot blade Front Kick

Chambering of the Front Pushing *Teep* Kick

A Foot-blade Front Stop kick

Front-leg Pushing Front Stop Kick against punching approach

Stopping a kick-chambering

Pushing Front Stop Kick to the knee of developing rear-leg Front Kick

Illustrative Photos

Front-leg Front Stop Kick to the thigh of a developing rear-leg Round-house Kick

Drilling the *Teep* Kick

  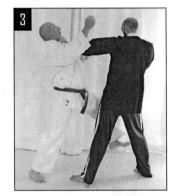

Compare a high Front Stop Kick to a Stop Jab: the principle is the same!

2. The Upward Front Stop Kick

Mae Geri Keage (general, Karatedo), Kin Geri (groin, Karatedo), Kinteki Sokushi Geri (groin, Nin Jitsu), Ago Kin Geri (chin, Nin Jitsu)

General

This is not a straight kick into the forward momentum of the attacker, and therefore it will not stop the attacker's body by itself. In order to be effective and actually stop an attack, this kick needs to target very sensitive areas of the body, and moreover, areas accessible from down under: the groin, the solar plexus, the throat, the chin or the armpit. It is a fast kick though, and if well-aimed, it is very useful and effective.

It is also a great kick to use in the "near-Stop Kick" situation described in the introduction: You kick after retreating just enough to cause your opponent to complete his attacking move while "just" falling short by an inch ("*Attack on Completion*", see next page).

Description

This is basically a regular Upward Front Kick, delivered usually with the front leg, with a hop (if necessary) or a hip push. See below.

Of course, again, the kick is conceivable as a rear-leg kick, as well as a switch kick, or after fancy evading footwork. Examples will be provided below and the first application describes a half-step retreat before delivery.

Front-leg Upward Front Stop Kick. Note the chamber and hip push

Key points

- This is not a power kick, but a *timing* kick: be fast and snappy

- Use your hips for distance: push your hips forward if you need some more range, keep straight if you do not. Make sure you surprise your opponent by going into the expected range or out of the centerline, or both.

- Remember that it is not a power kick: After kicking, get your body out of centerline immediately and follow up.

Targets

As mentioned, only sensitive points accessible upwards: throat, chin, solar plexus, groin and armpit of extended arm.

Typical application

The first series below shows the kick delivered to the armpit at *completion* of a full-step lunge punch by an opponent. The kick is delivered after half-a-step back with the front leg to place the body just out of range of the incoming punch.

The second series below shows the very simple and straightforward use of a rear-leg version of the kick to the groin of an attacker developing a rear-leg Roundhouse. Speed is of the essence, but it is actually easier than it looks.

Pull the front leg back and kick with right timing/distance

Rear-leg 'timing' Upward Front Stop Kick against a developing rear-leg Roundhouse

Specific training

- Drill lightly with an attacking—and protected—partner.

- Work the swinging bag. Of course, the bag must be hanging at groin level. Work at different ranges, rear- and front-leg-style, and with different foot-work patterns. The illustration at right shows a simple rear-leg version.

As the partner lets go of or throws the bag, aim to time-catch it from below when vertical

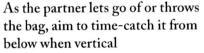

Self-defense

The figures that follow show the classic use of the kick against a Spin-back Hook Kick: Use your front leg to kick his groin as he spins back. Sweep his foot as it lands while pulling his shoulder down, and stomp-kick or downward-heel-kick him as he lands. The illustrations show clearly the cat-stance (*Neko Ashi Dachi – Karatedo*) position—with a weightless front leg—for easier and faster front-leg kicks. This position and its close cousins from all fighting arts are, of course, very important for front-leg stop-kicking. It should be noted here that, against trained opponents, the weightlessness of the front leg should be hidden as much as possible: it is an obvious tell-tale to the trained eye. The reader is invited to train, in front of the mirror, for a stance in which most of the weight is on the rear-leg without looking like it.

Timing Stop Kick to the groin; note the intermediate Cat Stance

This shows the kick used on an opponent fond of high Penetrating Front Kicks. If he uses his high Front Kicks as Stop Kicks, as is often the case, provoke him to execute with a convincing forward *head fake*. As he kicks, lean back to place your head and upper body out of range while kicking his groin. Even better: catch his foot at extension, and control it, or even lift it, as you kick. (A classic variation of this technique, less elegant but easier to perform, is catch-blocking the incoming kick, lifting the leg and *counter-kicking*).

Timing Groin Kick while leaning back

Here is an interesting slight variation on the same theme, but with a very hard finish. The chambering of your Front Kick is in itself a joint attack, and the follow-up is a tearing stretch typical of East-Asian Arts. As your assailant reacts to a feint with a Pushing Front Stop Kick, you retreat just enough to cause him to overreach. You catch his foot, preferably with a full fulcrum: the toes with the upper hand and the heel with the lower one. *While* catching, you are chambering your Front Stop Kick. It is preferable to develop an Inward-tilted version of the kick (as described in our book about *Essential Kicks*), a bit of a hybrid between a Front kick and a Small Roundhouse Kick. Your forceful kick chamber causes your knee to strike the knee joint of his caught leg that you are twisting and pulling on. You continue, *smoothly and without interruption*, to develop the kick in order to hit his exposed groin. As you chamber back, your kicking foot lands deeply rearwards, as you kneel and pull his leg forward to place him violently an into involuntary *Splits*-position. This technique is a very dangerous combination to be drilled slowly and carefully: you hurt the stretched knee joint, the exposed groin and then both the hip joint and the adductor muscles and ligaments.

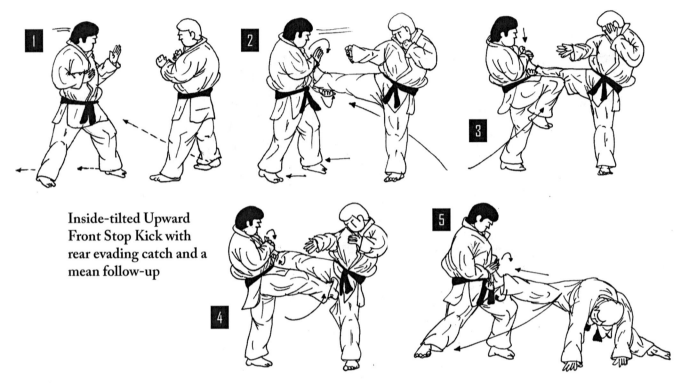

Inside-tilted Upward Front Stop Kick with rear evading catch and a mean follow-up

The sequence below shows a variation of this kick used against an opponent "shooting" for your legs in an attempted takedown. You pivot with your rear leg out of the centerline while controlling his neck with both hands. As soon as your leg is out of range, it starts a fast kick to the bent-over face, while you ideally still maintain downward pressure on his neck. The kick must be fast and direct, and therefore is somewhat of a straighter-leg kick and slightly "round-house" in its trajectory. It is still a Stop Kick, as the evasion and kick are smoothly uninterrupted and the momentum of his tackle attempt takes him into the kick.

On a tackle attempt, evade out and kick

Should you realize that your assailant is fond of counterpunches, here is a simple maneuver to teach him a good lesson. Remember that simplest is usually best! You simply fake a reverse punch or a cross, exaggerating the move, and especially exaggerating the hip twist. But you stop the hipped punch in mid-move and twist back, about when he starts the reverse punch your fake has caused. The front-leg Upward Front Kick should catch his groin at full punch extension. In any case, you are leaning back out of range as you kick. You can follow up with a front-leg sweep as he bends down on account of the Groin Kick.

Provoke a reverse punch that you will greet with a Groin Stop Kick

The Upward Front Stop Kick can be of use in a clinching situation where your opponent tries to attrite you with lateral Knee Strikes. Time your counter for the coming next knee strike, generally easy to detect by your opponent's body moves. As soon as he lifts his foot to strike, you strongly pivot into the strike while pulling his head powerfully downwards and into the twist. This sudden violent maneuver, just as he stands on one leg, will stop the Knee Strike and place him off-balance, directly into the trajectory of your own Upward Front Kick. This is not an orthodox clean Stop Kick, but certainly close enough, and very efficient. Follow up.

Twist and kick to stop a clinching lateral Knee Strike

A last example will be a near-Stop Kick, as mentioned before and as will also be explained in detail later in the text. The technique presented is not a clean classic Stop Kick, but a close relative in which a block, a catch and a kick are delivered nearly simultaneously. The distinction between Stop Kicks and Counter Kicks being sometimes very thin because of the circumstances, we shall discuss these close variations of Stop kicks in section 6. In the illustrations below, a wide swinging punch is blocked by evading forward and sideways into its development. The Scooping Block evolves naturally into a neck catch and simultaneous Upward Front Kick to the ribs of the assailant. According to the specific range, the impact could be with the shin, which is even better than with the toes or the top of the foot. The kick will help to bend him over and allow for the setting of a *Guillotine* front Neck Lock. This is not a classic Stop Kick, but the forward evasion/block/catch/*kick* maneuver is certainly a 'timing' stopping technique.

A close relative: simultaneous evading catch-Block and Stop Kick

Illustrative Photos

Upward Front Stop Kick against a punch – *Itay Leibovitch*

The Essential Upward Front Kick to the armpit

Upward Groin Front Stop Kick against developing Round-house

Evading "timing" Upward Front Stop Kick against Front Kick

Drilling the classic Upward Front Kick

Back-Side Stop Kick in free-fighting– *Roy Faige*

Kin Geri: classic Essential Upward Front Kick to the groin

3. The Side Pushing Kick and other Side Stop Kicks

Yoko Sokutei Osae Uke (Karatedo)

General

This is the 'Side' version of the Pushing Kick, and most of what was said about the Front Pushing Kick is relevant. This is a fast but less powerful Side Kick, aimed at stopping the incoming body of an attacker. It is mainly a front-leg kick, much more so than the Front Pushing Kick, because of the hip position. This is a great Stop Kick though, especially if you are standing in a side position guard. It is used against the whole body or incoming legs of an opponent. It is very common in point tournament fighting, where—being fast—it can score points even as an attack-kick, although it is not as powerful as a real Side Kick should be. It is even sometimes used to push the opponent out of the fighting area limits to cause him penalty points. Of course, this is not our purpose here: We shall describe it as the fantastic Stop Kick it is.

Side Stop Kick in free fighting – *Ziv Faige*

Key points

- Despite its "pushing" side, the kick must mentally and physically be delivered as much as possible as a *kick*, and not as a push.

- Always chamber back before lowering the leg.

- Always push the hips into the kick, as you could be against very serious momentum. The main positive attribute of all Side Kicks is the power of the hip thrust.

Description

Just like for the Front Pushing Kick, the difference between the classic Essential Penetrating Side Kick and the Side Pushing Kick is in the chamber position: the Figure below shows clearly that the chamber of the Pushing Kick (below) is already half-way on its trajectory, in order to place the foot immediately between you and your opponent. All the principles are, from this point on, identical to those of a classic Side Kick, including hip position and the chambering back of the kicking leg.

Comparative chambering position of classic and Pushing Side kick: end-position is identical

Of course, matters of timing and distance make it necessary to adapt, and the kick must sometimes be delivered with a small hop (See Figure at right). The illustrations below show even the extreme of a forward-flying version of the kick against a rear-leg Full Roundhouse attack. This is a logical principle of a shorter *straight-line* stop versus a longer *circular* attack! But you can also beat a straight attack by being faster than your opponent or by coming from *above* his kick, as shown in the photos below.

The hopping Side Pushing Stop Kick

The "long and low" front-leg flying version of the Side Pushing Stop Kick

Flying Side Stop Kick against a straight Front Kick

Targets

As a rule of thumb—just like for the Front Pushing Kick—you should target the center of the body, close to the gravity center, in order to ensure the stopping of your opponent; aim for the solar plexus, the lower belly, the ribs and the hips.

If your proficiency and the circumstances allow for it, you can go for more specific targets like the throat, the armpit and the groin.

The upper legs are always a good target, as they will generally stop the forward movement (right).

Side Pushing Stop Kick to the thigh

Typical application

The series below shows the classic "timing" use against a Reverse Punch. You stop-kick, in-place, with the front leg. Follow up with a *rebounding* high Roundhouse Kick from the same leg for example.

Side Stop Kick against punch, *in place*

These two photos show, again, a front-leg "timing" use against a punch, but this time with a small hop forward to catch the opponent at the very beginning of his combination move.

Side Stop Kick against punch,
hopping forward

This sequence shows a slightly later delivery of the Stop Kick (closer to an "*Attack on delivery*") against a faster jab. You bend back to avoid the jab and then stop-kick. You can follow up with a same-leg rebounding high Hook Kick.

Side Stop Kick against punch, *in place after leaning back*

Last but not least, the Figures below show a 'step-away' version of the Side Stop Kick. As the opponent lunges with a jab, you are too late for a forward-going Stop Kick; you rather step away with your rear leg before lifting the now-free front leg into a "Side Stop Kick-chamber". After side-kicking your opponent's open ribs, you can follow up with a full-power 'Low Kick' from your other leg.

Side Stop Kick against punch, *after step-away*

The Figures below show the use of the kick for stopping your opponent's own developing front-leg Side Kick by targeting his hip joint. This is a 'timing' Kick that makes use of the extra time needed by the attacker to develop a "real" fully-powered Side Kick; it also builds on his expectation of your instinctive retreat instead of your forward thrust. Follow up!

Side stop-kick the hip of a developing kick

Specific training

- Partner drilling! More partner drilling!

- This kick is very important and needs a lot of practice, from all possible ranges, against a swinging bag thrown at you by a partner.

Self defense

As already shown above, this is a great Stop Kick against punches, as you kick the ribs exposed by the developing punch. This sequence shows an important close range application of the kick, requiring less hip thrust. Against a jab, you control the incoming hand while push-kicking into the exposed ribs. Keep control of the hand while lowering the leg and attack your assailant's throat. You can follow up with a Groin Kick.

Simultaneous Stop Kick and block/catch

The Figures below show the classic use against a Spin-back attack, already presented with the Front Pushing Kick. The Spin-back could be the start of any attack, Hook Kick or Hammer-fist Punch. In this example, you target the assailant's lower back as he spins back; you then lower the foot close to him and you catch his hair and shoulder (head and throat are also possibilities). Pull him down powerfully onto your bent front knee while crouching. Needless to mention that this is a very dangerous technique.

Front-leg Pushing Side Stop Kick against Spin-back attack

The series below shows the use of the Side Stop Kick when you take the initiative by luring your assailant into a counter. In this classic tactical "trap" set-up, you attack your opponent with a high Jab/Cross combination. After the cross (*Jodan Gyacku Tsuki – Karatedo*), you pull back, but not too far and with your hands slightly down, in order to entice a natural high punch counterattack. Your pull-back has freed your front leg which is already coming up in Side Stop Kick-chamber; kick just as he punches, and then follow up!

Provoke a counterattack in order to stop-kick his ribs

This sequence shows the use of the kick against a "shoot" attempt. This kick variation is delivered lower, on a bent standing leg, and with a more upwards trajectory. You have noticed your opponent's propensity to feint high before rushing for the tackle. As he moves in again, just lift the front leg in a Side Stop Kick-chamber, placing all your weight fast on the *bent* rear leg. Kick at his lowered throat level. If you have taken care of minimal telegraphing, he will impale himself on the kick.

Painful foil of a take-down attempt

Illustrative Photos

The basic Essential Penetrating Side Kick

A Side Stop Kick

Compare the chambers for a basic Side Kick and a Pushing Side Stop Kick

Classic Chamber position for Pushing Side Stop Kick

High Side Stop Kick application in self-defense"

The Side Stop Kick is also very efficient when delivered to the legs, as will be shown in the next section

Stopping a developing Side Kick

A Side Stop Kick

Illustrative Photos

Lean-back Pushing Side Stop Kick against a puncher; striking the ribs opened by the punch

Stopping a combination attack that starts with a distance-closing back-fist strike

The "back" version of the Side Stop Kick, nearly a Back Kick. The kick can be shorter or longer according to the relative positions

Perfect 'timing' high Side Stop Kick in tournament – *Marc De Bremaeker*

4. The Low Side Stop Kick

General

The Low Side Stop Kick is a regular Low Side Kick; regular in the sense that it is not a *Push* Kick. The target being the opponent's leg, there is enough time to chamber, at least partly, and to deliver a full-fledged kick. The Low Side Stop Kick is also the *Obstruction* Kick par excellence: whether you are attacking or stop-kicking, a kick to the legs tends to totally disrupt any possible effective move by the opponent. This is also probably the kick of choice in *Bruce Lee's Jeet Kune Do* system, and not without reason: it is powerful, versatile and extremely effective, especially in its "timing" version.

The reader is invited to consult our previous book '*Low Kicks*' for further reading about the Low Side kick and its variations.

But to sum it up, this is definitely a kick to master.

Description

As presented, this is very simply a Low Side Kick, with some chambering, delivered at the right moment to make it a Stop Kick. The first series below shows its delivery, in place, with a full chamber.

The second series shows an example of the hopping forward-version of the kick, which allows for much less chambering.

Above: Full-chamber front-leg Low Side Stop Kick

Right: Minimal-chamber front-leg hopping Side Stop Kick

The Figures below show the delivery as an *Obstruction against* a hopping front-leg full Side Kick. Please note the high hand move for momentum and to misdirect the opponent's attention away from the low kick for as long as possible. The fact that you go forward instead of retreating will allow you to foil his range calculations and stop his kick as it only starts to chamber. In fact, you can condition him by retreating a few times on his attacks before executing the stop-technique.

Front-leg hopping "obstruction" Low Side Stop Kick against a full Hopping Kick

This sequence shows the use of the kick as an *Obstruction* Kick again, but while <u>*attacking*</u>. This is still a Stop Kick, as you hop forward *as soon as* you feel the opponent's decision to commit to an attack (*Sen no sen*). As soon as your kick has connected, take control of his lead hand and jab to the chin. Your move delivers a painful kick, gets his attention down as you prepare to punch high, and prevents any starting kick, any Stop Kick, any step or any meaningful footwork. Make sure you follow up.

Offensive Obstruction Low Side Stop Kick to close the distance"

Targets

Preferably the knee itself, from any side. Other possibilities are the shin, ankle and lower thigh.

Specific training

- Train with a partner, but be very careful with knee attacks.

- Practice on a used tire held in place by a partner and simulating a knee. You can kick a few inches into the target. Deliver from all *ranges* and hopping forward and backwards. Train for speed, on the random "go" of your partner (See below). You must 'role-play' the sudden stopping aspect of this kick.

Key points

- As mentioned, always chamber at least minimally, and always chamber back.

- Do not push, kick!

- Keep your hands up (You are close!) and always follow up.

The best target for drilling this kick: the tire

Typical application

The Figures below show the typical application against a step-forward—in this case, a stepping Lunge Punch. This kick is both a momentum-stopper and a knee-damaging kick. Aim for the knee and kick through. "Stick" to your opponent as he is thrown off-balance backwards, and follow up with a back-fist. Keep the pressure on—in this example with a sweep.

Side stop-kick the incoming knee as he steps forward to attack; lean back as a precaution

Here is an application of the kick as an offensive *distance-closer and Obstruction Kick*. The following combination presented is for the flexible fast high-kicker, but nearly any other follow-up would be applicable. As your opponent *gets ready* to attack, you hop forward and stop-kick his forward knee. You chamber up for a *Double* Roundhouse Kick follow-up: roundhouse-kick his groin directly, without lowering the foot (In a sport configuration you kick the abdomen); you then follow up by using the same leg to roundhouse-kick his leaning head (whether your foot touches the floor first or not will depend on your level of proficiency). This is an important classic combination requiring serious training, and therefore an excellent drill in itself.

Triple Kick combination starting with a hopping obstruction front-leg Low Side Stop Kick

Self defense

As mentioned, stop-kicking is also stopping and attacking *limbs* directly. This sequence shows an additional application of the kick against a Side or Back Kick, from opposite stances: You stop-kick the back of the knee of the attacking leg as it lifts off the floor. If you think about it, this is identical to the application presented above but, in this case, your opponent's kick is caught later in its development. Again, the whole move is based on the miscalculation of distance by your assailant: You hop forward instead of retreating as expected. Follow up with a fully powered high Roundhouse Kick for instance.

Intercept the developing Side Kick and follow up

This series shows another "*stop-the-attacking-limb*" application: stop-kick the knee of a chambering rear-leg Front Kick. Control his lead hand as you land, and follow up, for example with a high reverse punch, and a subsequent 'Low Kick'.

Intercept the chambering rear-leg Front Kick and follow up

And last, but not least, an additional, but more "self-defense" illustration of the use of the kick against a forward-stepping attack. As an assailant steps forward to hit you with a stick, you unexpectedly hop forward instead of cowering back, and you stop-kick the knee of his stepping leg. You can follow up with a 'Low kick' (below).

Hop forward and side-stop-kick his front leg as he steps forward while lifting his stick overhead

Illustrative Photos

Three illustrations of the classical Low Side Kick

Low Side Stop Kick to the standing leg of a kicker

Timing nuance for the Low Side Stop Kick: stop the kicking hop or stop the lifting leg

Obstruction Low Side Kick to close the distance safely

Stopping a hopping front-leg Side Kick in its tracks

Low Side Stop Kick as an offensive obstruction kick

5. The 'Timing' Low Roundhouse Kick

General

As we were dealing with Low Kicks, here comes the Low Roundhouse Stop Kick. This is a kick that cannot stop the forward momentum of an attacker. It is fast, but also circular, low and lacking in power. To work as a Stop Kick, it will be entirely dependent on precise timing and accuracy: it must hit sensitive targets only, and at the right time. When so delivered—fast, accurately and at the right moment—it is a very effective kick. It is also an important kick to master, before starting to train for the *high* 'timing' Roundhouse Kick coming next. Proficiency will come mostly by partner-training, as power is not of the essence. Note that, because of its lack of forward power, this kick is often delivered together with centerline-evasion and/or upper body-bending (away); examples will be given in the text.

Key points

- The kick must be fast and accurate. No need to concentrate on power, but rather on speed.

- Kick a few inches *into* the target, and chamber back: this is a "whipping" kick.

- Always follow up.

- When possible, always bend or lean your upper body away from the attack.

Targets

Only the knee—from all sides—and the groin.

Description

The kick is simply an Essential Low Roundhouse to the *knee* or the *groin*. It is generally a front-leg kick with some forward thrust: at least a hip push, but more often a small hop. It is delivered as soon as the opponent is set onto launching his own attack. To succeed with this kick, it is important to go *forward* in order to foil the opponent's attack plan, and especially his range-closing expectations.

Specific training

This kick must be drilled for speed, timing and precision. Not power:

- Train with a protected partner attacking you at random.

- Work on a *marked* heavy bag or tire from various distances for range control, no-telegraphing start and target precision.

Timing Groin Roundhouse Stop Kick

Typical application

This series shows the classic use of the kick against an opponent hopping forward, for a full-powered front-leg Kick: As he expects you to retreat, you hop forward and roundhouse-kick his groin. Note the upper body leaning away to avoid possible punches. Follow up; low-kick (Straight-leg Low Roundhouse Kick) with the other leg for example. The combination will work best if you first mis-condition him by retreating exaggeratedly a few times from his front-leg attacks.

Timing Low Roundhouse Stop Kick works extremely well against long-hopping kicks

The Figures below show the typical stop-kicking of a *stepping* leg: You have to 'time-hit' the knee before the step is complete! The example, against a full-step Lunge Punch, shows how to slightly evade the centerline while kicking his knee just before the step is complete. Get control of the punching hand if possible. The kick will both be very painful and put him off-balance. Spin-back into a low Hook Kick to the same knee to throw him down. Keep kicking him as he lands.

Time the Roundhouse to the knee as his foot lands for the step-punch; but this is a kick, not a sweep!

Self defense

This will show an atypical 'cutting' application using the *rear* leg. Note that it is based on a full evasion from the centerline. As your attacker starts a forward-hopping front-leg Roundhouse Kick, you lunge away from the center-line and deliver, below his kicking leg, a rear-leg body-bent Roundhouse Stop Kick to the knee of his standing leg.

Evading moves will allow for rear-leg Stop Kicks

Of course, the same cutting technique can be executed with the front leg; the timing must be perfect and it is also important to smother the high kick impact with the shoulder and arm while delivering the Cutting Stop Kick.

Front-leg Low Roundhouse Stop Kick to the standing leg; the attacking high Roundhouse is well controlled by the shoulder and front arm

The Figures below show an important self-defense maneuver: The *Preventive* Low Roundhouse Kick to the knee. When the aggressive intentions of an assailant are clear, the earlier you strike, the better… As he starts moving to-wards you, you hop forward instead of retreating as he expects, and you kick his forward knee, preferably just as his foot lands. As mentioned, always follow up; in this example, by controlling his armed elbow and hammer-punching his exposed ribs, and then catching his head for a downward twist to knee strike. You can continue by pushing him away to allow for a Groin Upward Front Kick. And more…

Always adequate on an opponent stepping forward: hopping towards him with a front-leg Roundhouse Stop Kick to the incoming knee

What is true for the knee is even truer for the groin. As soon as an assailant reveals his aggressive intentions, do not wait for him to take the initiative and do not retreat. Surprise him by hopping forward and kick his groin at the very beginning of his offensive, as early as possible. And make sure there is no telegraphing of your pre-emptive intentions. The Figures that follow show such an example against a stick-wielding assailant: Kick as soon as you 'feel' that he starts lifting his stick.

Hopping Groin Kick as the assailant
lifts his stick; follow up with a Low Kick.
Always stand your ground

The Low Roundhouse Kick can be used as a Cutting Kick against a knee strike attempt in a clinch situation. Lateral knee strikes are extremely common in the clinching matches of MMA or *Muay Thai* fights. It is also a potential real-life situation, and the following kick can be a great help against an avid kneeing enthusiast. The key for the success of this technique is placing your assailant off-balance just at the right moment: as he lifts his foot for another knee strike. You then twist him forcefully and slightly downwards towards his lifting knee, all the while delivering a Roundhouse Kick to his *standing* knee. The moves must be simultaneous; the upper body twists one way to pull the opponent, and the hips twist the other way to pull the kick. Aim for the knee as precisely as possible.

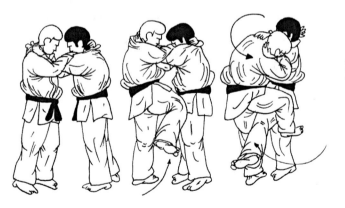

A Cutting Low Roundhouse Stop
Kick against a clinched knee strike

Illustrative Photos

Typical Essential Low Roundhouse Kicks

The favorite Kick of "hard" fighting Arts

Typical "timing" Low Roundhouse Stop Kicks

The Groin 'timing' Roundhouse Stop Kick will cut a forward hop short!

The Low Roundhouse Stop Kick as a Cutting Kick

Illustrative Photos

The 'timing' Groin Roundhouse Stop Kick, respectively against a jab and against a reverse punch

Stop-kicking a front chamber

Marc De Bremaeker in tournament: Stop-kicking developing kick

6. The 'Timing' Roundhouse Kick, Other Roundhouse Stop Kicks and Near-Stop Kicks

General

Just like the previous low version, the *'timing'* Roundhouse Stop Kick is simply a Roundhouse Kick delivered at the right moment. Just like the previous kick, it does not come head-on towards the forward momentum of your attacker. It is not a straight Stop Kick, and to be effective, it needs perfect timing and accuracy in hitting a sensitive target. It is one of my favorite kicks though—extremely effective when well-delivered—and it was my signature technique (*Tokui Waza*) at the beginning of my competing career. It is a head kick generally—although the solar plexus is also a viable target—and it is generally delivered with the front leg and some kind of forward move. Moreover, when possible, the preferred version should be a 'body-bent' or 'hand-on-floor' version of the Hopping Roundhouse Kick.

Key points

*   Timing Kicks must be first and foremost fast and accurate; power attributes come only after those prerequisites.

*   Always tend to hop or stretch forward for a maximum disruption of the expected range of attack by the opponent.

*   Always follow up.

*   Kick a few inches into the target and chamber back: This is a *whip* kick.

Description

There is not much to describe: this is a regular Essential *High* Roundhouse Kick, usually front-leg. Our previous work about Essential Kicks contains a whole chapter about Roundhouse Kicks: there are many variations to the basic execution, and most of them are applicable to 'timing' stop-kicking. The reader is invited to consult this treatise for more about roundhouse-kicking. The applications we shall present here will be more specifically Stop Kicks.

It should be mentioned that the kick is conceivable as a rear-leg Kick, as an Essential *Switch* Kick for example, or even simply as a powerful rear-leg Roundhouse aimed at forcefully disrupt the incoming attack. The kick could even be a powerful rear-leg *Straight-leg* version (The Essential *'Low Kick'*), as illustrated below. As mentioned many times, all kicks can become Stop Kicks.

It is important to remember, that—as a head kick with the aim to stop an attack in its tracks—it is preferable that the kick comes from the opponent's inside: a kick coming from his outside could be blocked by his elevated shoulder, inadvertently or purposefully.

Rear-leg Straight-leg Roundhouse Stop Kick against Spin-back Elbow Strike

Targets

Preferably the head (and groin described in the previous section).

Eventually the solar plexus or the kidneys, if you are proficient and also can connect with the ball of the foot (or a shoe tip).

Typical application

The illustration below shows the hopping forward delivery of the kick as the opponent prepares to hop forward for his own front-leg Kick. Of course, it works best if you have lured your opponent into believing you shall retreat from his hopping kicks by preceding behavior. I suppose some of the more skeptical readers will have some doubts about the realism of this technique. I can assure them that this is a highly effective technique, when executed properly and after much drilling. This was one of my favorites when I was a karate points-fighter and it brought me many successes: As soon as my opponent would start moving (expecting to have to close the distance), my Roundhouse was in his face. The critics could still try to emphasize the points-Karate aspect and argue that the kick lacks power. It is true that the kick needs to be fast and lacks power, but many of those I delivered back then caused knock-downs and even light knock-outs because they were totally unexpected by the opponent. And remember that you should always follow-up…

The redoubtable "timing" front-leg hopping-forward High Roundhouse Stop Kick

If you have not been fast enough to catch your opponent early in his attack, you still can lean back (Refer to the Essential Body-bent Roundhouse Kick) while kicking *in place* from the front leg. The Figures below show the use of an 'in-place' version of the kick, while evading a punch by bending back and lowering the head and body away. The top Figure evades a jab in same stances and the bottom Figure evades a cross in *opposite* stances: Remember the important notion that a head kick should generally be delivered on the inside of the attacker, so as not to stumble ineffectively into a raised shoulder.

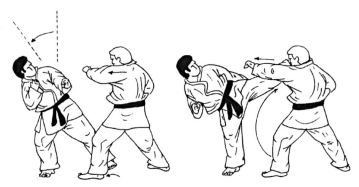

In-place front-leg high Roundhouse Stop Kick against a jab

In-place front-leg high Roundhouse Stop Kick against a reverse punch

An interesting special variation of this Stop Kick is presented in the following figures. The chambering of the Roundhouse is used as a *Leg Block* from which the kick will proceed. This special variation is surprisingly efficient, especially against Front Kicks. The Knee Block will hurt, will cause deviation of the kick trajectory and will place the attacker off-balance; all this will more than compensate for the fact that the kick is inherently less powerful than the basic Roundhouse Stop Kick.

Leg Block with a chambered Roundhouse Stop Kick

Specific training

- All "timing" Kicks must be practiced with a partner; there is no other way. Your partner should be protected (groin protection and training helmet) or he should hold a focus pad.

- Free-fight with one of the partners trying, from time to time only, stop-kicking (See below).

- Drill your speed and accuracy on a marked swinging bag (See right).

- Drill in front of the mirror for a no tell-tale delivery and for the explosiveness of the maneuver.

Drilling the Roundhouse Stop Kick on a swinging bag; start from various ranges and aim for precision

High Roundhouse Stop Kick in free-fighting

Self defense

Illustrated below is the use of the Roundhouse Stop Kick against the recently brought-back-to-fashion Flying Knee Strike, typical of *Muay Thai* or modern MMA fights. In this application, it is better to get slightly out of the way with an evading 'out-and-forward' step; the fast Hopping Roundhouse Stop Kick will then blend in smoothly to catch the assailant still airborne. Follow up.

Evade slightly out of the trajectory of the Flying Knee Strike and stop-kick

The series at right shows the classic use of the Essential *Body-bent* version of the kick to evade a regular high Roundhouse while scoring with what is basically the same kick. In this example, your assailant is fond of high kicks, as you have noticed by retreating a few times to get a feel of his skills. This time, as he starts forward, so do you. In this example, the Stop Kick goes all the way down to the Essential *Hand-on-floor* version of the front-leg Roundhouse Kick, which puts your body safely away from his own kick. Timing is, of course, of the essence; and follow-up is a requisite, as in any self-defense situation.

Front-leg "timing" Roundhouse Stop Kick with body evasion

The next series of Figures show the classical delivery from *opposite* stances, against a rear-leg Front Kick. Hop forward and slightly out of the centerline as soon as your assailant's move starts. You can then land in a foot stomp and follow up with a Back-fist and an opposite direction Spin-back Hook Kick.

Front-leg 'timing' Kick against rear-leg chambering of Front Kick: You need to be fast

The Figure at right shows the use of a regular full *rear-leg* Roundhouse, in a "*Sen-no-sen*" situation. You may look like the aggressor, but your assailant's own attack was about to start; after some training, you'll know when this happens. Your assailant is openly aggressive, and you do not wait for him to concretize his attack: do not look defiant, but as soon as he decides to step forward, kick with full commitment. Follow up.

Preventive strike, just as your opponent starts to get into attack mode…The ultimate Stop-Kick"

Another typical rear-leg Stop Kick is the Essential <u>Switch</u> Kick: you switch legs more or less in place to allow for a more powerful rear-leg Kick with what *was* your front leg. This allows for small distance adjustments, range assessment jamming and… surprise. The switch version of the basic kicks is very useful and sneakily disconcerting; I warmly recommend its use, though parsimoniously. In the sequence below, you deal with an assailant fond of the 'Reverse punch/rear-leg Front Kick' combo as an opener of his combinations. As he starts, you switch legs while adjusting your distance a little bit rearwards. Your originally-front leg "rebounds" on the floor as it lands rearwards and develops a full-power rear-leg high Roundhouse Kick that will catch him in mid-move. Follow up, with a Spin-back Hook Kick for example.

The more powerful rear-leg Switch-type Roundhouse Stop-Kick

The Straight-leg version of the Roundhouse 'timing' Stop Kick is of particular advantage in close combat situations, and therefore in self-defense. As soon as your opponent "opens" his ribs for a strike, you can stop-kick him. If, for example and as illustrated, your assailant is a heavy user of the Spin-back Horizontal Elbow strike—*Muay Thai* style—you can slightly lean back while executing a punishing Straight-leg Roundhouse Stop Kick to his very exposed

Muay Thai-style Stop Kick against Muay Thai-style attack

Illustrative Photos

Illustration of High Roundhouse Stop-Kicks in actual use

The Essential basic High Roundhouse Kick

High Roundhouse Stop-Kick in actual tournament – *Marc De Bremaeker*

Essential *Hand-on-floor* **version of the High Roundhouse Kick**

Illustration of the Essential *Downward* **version of the Round-house Kick**

Classic High Roundhouse Kick in free-fighting

Illustrative Photos

High 'timing' Roundhouse Stop Kick, with evasion, against kick

There is no alternative to partner training for Stop-kicking progress

High 'timing' Roundhouse Stop Kick against stepping opponent

Alternate view of the evading 'timing' High Roundhouse Kick, against kick and punching step

Timing high Roundhouse Stop Kick in tournament – *Marc De Bremaeker*

Two more examples of 'timing' Roundhouse Stop Kicks

Near-Stop Kicks

As mentioned in the introduction, stop-kicking is not an exact science and there are many small variations of timing possible. It is difficult to define a Stop Kick with precision, as it could be delivered as soon as the opponent has decided to attack, and as late as after you have evaded his attack. The Roundhouse Kick being a workhorse of fighting Arts, the author found it suitable to give in this section a few examples of techniques that are not fully *Stop Kicks* by orthodox definition, but still very close. The reader will draw his own conclusions and adapt these maneuvers to other kicks. The introduction details a few categories of Stop Kicks and Near-Stop Kicks, and the interested reader should refer back to those lines. The experienced Artist will also understand that there are intermediate stages in the techniques presented, and different possible emphasis to give, closer or further from classic stop-kicking. One should chose to drill and use what is most suitable to his morphology, to his previous training and to his psychological affinities.

An example of a close relative of Stop Kicks is presented below; it is a Roundhouse *Counter* Kick after <u>evading and controlling</u> a kicking attack. This can be considered a near-Stop Kick because the Roundhouse Kick impacts *before* your assailant's foot is back on the floor.

Evade back;
Control and
redirect attacking
leg; Kick landing
opponent

Another quasi-Stop Kick would be a <u>rearwards one-step evasion</u>, with the foot which you pulled back *rebounding* on the floor into a Stop Kick. In the example below, you evade a full powered kick-through Roundhouse Kick by retreating by a full step back. But, as soon as the kick has passed, your formerly front leg bounces back forward for a Straight-leg Roundhouse Kick to the opponent's midsection. As his kicking leg has not fully landed yet, this can be, again, considered a very close relative of a Stop Kick.

A full rearwards evading step rebounds instantly into a powerful Stop Kick

Of course, it may sometimes be enough to <u>lean back</u> as an evasive maneuver with no extra need to step back or move the feet at all. Sometimes leaning back with a small half-step will be enough; the idea is a movement of the intended target (head, body or leg) just long enough to place it out of range, but not more. You can then counter-kick while his attacking leg is still airborne, which is, again, very close to a real Stop Kick. In the example below, upper body leaning will place the head out of the range of the opponent's high front-leg Hopping Side Kick. Your own Roundhouse Counter Kick could catch him even before his kicking foot can land.

Evade opponent's kick by leaning back; Initiate Counter Kick as soon as he start chambering back

The following technique is a bit further away from the real Stop Kick: You kick while <u>catching his leg</u>. The ideal execution is kicking and catching simultaneously; and please believe me that it is very possible if your opponent has become predictable or if your senses have been well-honed. Of course, the maneuver works well even if you catch first and kick immediately afterwards. In this example, you move into his mid-level Roundhouse Kick in order to smother it while catching and immobilizing his leg. As simultaneously as possible, hop into a front-leg Roundhouse Kick to the knee of his standing leg.

Catch a kicking leg and counter-kick

Of course, all these near-Stop Kick techniques are not only valid for kicking assailants but can be adapted to a *punching* opponent. The Figures below show the "rebounding" leg-technique after the evasion from a Reverse Punch. The evasion is—in this instance—a 90 degrees pivot on the front leg while the rear leg does a quarter of a circle back to take the body out of the centerline (This is the classic Ju-Jitsu and Aikido's *Tai Sabaki*). The rear leg rebounds back at once for a Roundhouse Kick to the opened ribs of the attacker.

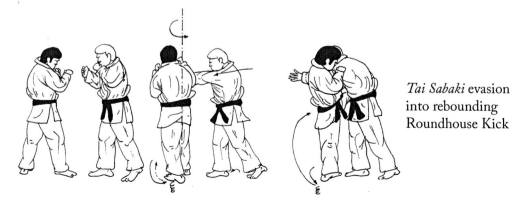

Tai Sabaki evasion into rebounding Roundhouse Kick

The parallel to the controlled-leg Counter Kick could be something like the techniques presented in the following illustrations. As your opponent launches his Cross Punch, you lean sideways while delivering your own Reverse Punch over his extending arm—sort of a bobbing/ducking maneuver. While he is so controlled, your rear-leg Roundhouse Kick is already on the way.

Evade sideways while controlling the incoming punch; then kick

If you are in opposite stances, you can evade the Cross Punch by stepping *forward and out* in a classic outside evasion; you can control the developing punch if needed. The Stop Kick is on its way as soon as your stepping foot lands. Without the controlling block, this classic technique would be a clean evading Roundhouse Stop Kick; the block or control is just an extra safety that makes this kick a quasi-Stop Kick.

Evading-out Roundhouse Stop Kick with control

Should you fully <u>block</u> an attack—an incoming Front Kick for example—and then execute a Counter Kick, it would take you further away from the clean Stop Kick. But if it is all done smoothly and fast, so that the Counter Kick is connecting before the original kicking foot of the assailant even lands, we are still very close to stop-kicking. In the illustration below, the half-step back with downward block (*Gedan Barai – Karatedo*) is blending into the start of the Near-Stop Kick.

Another close relative of Stop Kicks: block and swiftly kick

Even further away from the clean Stop Kick, would be the examples below of an <u>Evade/Block/Catch/Set up</u> and then kick. As your opponent attacks with a rear-leg Roundhouse or Front Kick, you block while evading out; your downward Block becomes a scoop that ultimately places the caught leg of your opponent onto your shoulder. Even if flexible, your opponent is in a difficult position and under your control. You can get even better control by stepping closer and using your front hand to catch the back of his neck to pull it forward. In order to get there, you may need to soften him up with a punch or a palm strike. From there, you could follow up with a low Hook Kick to the calf of his standing leg which would also cause him to fall down. Or—in a more serious confrontation—you could deliver a low Front Kick to his standing leg with the dual purpose of both hurting him and furthering his foot even more; your kicking foot is then pulled powerfully rearwards while you kneel down in order to forcefully stretch your opponent into involuntary 'Splits'. This is a very dangerous technique that must be practiced extremely carefully.

Block, Scoop, Catch, Set up, Kick to takedown

Illustrative Photo: Timing Round-house Stop Kick in free-fighting against *Rui Monteiro*

Block, Scoop, Catch, Set up, Kick to dangerous tearing stretch

7. The 'Timing' Roundhouse to Pushing Side Kick

General

This kick could have been categorized as a *Double Kick* or a *Feint Kick*; it is basically a combination: a high Roundhouse Kick blending into a same-leg Side Kick to the body. In spite of being complex, it is an important maneuver for the assiduous stop-kicker. The way it is presented here can turn this combination into a Stop Kick, in two ways: 1) The high Roundhouse is a "timing" Stop Kick, followed by a same-leg Side Kick, *the purpose of which is to make sure the opponent's forward momentum is stopped.* 2) The Roundhouse Kick is an offensive kick, a prodding kick or a "light" Stop Kick; but in all three cases *its purpose is to* draw *the opponent into a counterattack that will be* Side-Stop-kicked. No matter how you look at it, it is a Stop Kick. It should be noted that the transition between the two basic kicks of the combination is exceedingly natural to a trained Artist, and therefore this is also an important combination to drill for general kicking speed, hip flexibility, and kicking self-assuredness.

Description

These Figures show the use of the combination as a classic "timing" Stop Kick: as soon as your opponent's attack starts to take form, you hop forward with the fast high Roundhouse. Chamber back and, from the chamber position, smoothly deliver a Side Kick to the mid-body as he starts to react. The Side Kick is both a follow-up and an insurance of having stopped his forward momentum at its very start.

A double Stop Kick, for good measure

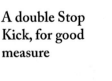

Key points

- This is one uninterrupted move: Do not stop between kicks.

- Key to success is the speed and "whippiness" of the first kick.

- If necessary, you can bend away when delivering the side kick to further remove your head and upper body from danger.

- The Roundhouse Kick best comes from the opponent's inside, so as not to be eventually hindered by his shoulder. An alternative is to use the "downward" version of the Roundhouse Kick.

Targets

- For the Roundhouse Kick, groin or face exclusively in this combination.

- For the Side Kick, around his center of gravity: ribs, lower belly, hips. The thighs and knees are also great targets to stop his momentum.

Typical application

The Figures below show the use of the technique as an "*Attack by Drawing*" tactic. In that specific case, the high Roundhouse Kick can come from the opponent's outside, as it is not imperative that it fully scores. You attack your opponent with a convincing hopping front-leg high Roundhouse Kick that he will block or absorb; this is best executed after a few 'failed' similar hopping Roundhouses that will give him confidence. As he starts his counterattack—in this case a reverse punch—you chamber back and get into Side Kick chamber. In this example, we have gone all the way to an even more powerful Essential *Back* Side Kick. After side-kicking his open ribs, you can follow up with a back-fist, and more.

Specific training

- Of course drill with a partner. This is the right place to introduce drilling with protective gear (below).

- Drill the Roundhouse all the way to the Side Kick-chamber for speed, ten times each leg. Then repeat, but stop for 1 second in chambered position, and follow by hopping and side kicking with power. Repeat ten times each leg.

- Drill the basic Double Kick on a marked (2 levels: head & groin) heavy bag. Then have a partner swing it towards you for the Stop Kick-effect.

Drill with a partner in protective gear: lightly kick his head and have him try to counterattack in earnest

1

Lure your opponent into a counterattack that you will stop-kick

2

3

4

5

6

Illustrative Photos

Stop his attack with a 'timing' Roundhouse, push him away with a Side Kick

8.   The Spin-back Side Stop Kick

General

Spin-back straight kicks are great kicks for stop-kicking: They add the energy of the spin to the energy of the kick and to the energy of the opponent's forward momentum. This makes it clear that Spin-back straight Kicks are "momentum-stoppers". The Spin-back Side Stop Kick is therefore very effective; as it is generally directed to the mid-body, it tends to do a lot of damage, as the opponent is usually extended and uncovered on account of his attack. The kick is a very close relative of the Spin-back Back Stop Kick, and whether to use one or the other is a matter of personal affinity and preferences. Often, the boundary between the two kicks is blurred by hybrid versions. Both are important to practice, and they are, in the author's opinion, the orthodox Stop Kicks *par excellence*.

Spin-back Side Stop Kick in free-fighting

Key points

- Spin back with the head and shoulders first, letting them pull the hips into the kick.

- Make sure you stop the circular spin-back movement *before* you start the straight kick delivery. This is the basic theory of the Essential Spin-back Side Kick and other straight Spin-back Kicks, as detailed in previous work.

- It is always preferable to bend the upper body, to keep it away from danger and help the kick.

- Thrust the hips into the kick. It is important for all Side Kicks, but even more when they are Stop Kicks.

- Always chamber back and follow up.

Description

The kick is very simply a classic *Essential* Spin-back Side Kick, as described in previous work. What makes it a Stop Kick is the timing and the opportunity. According to the type of attack, the spin-back can be executed in place, slightly retreating or going a bit forward. But you should always strive to deliver it as a "*Sen-no-sen*" kick, spinning-back with a forward surge, as soon as you "feel" the opponent's attack building up. Again, it could then probably look as if you are the attacker, and not the other way around.

The Figures below show the classic but less optimal delivery of the kick, as your opponent is already starting his full-step Lunge Punch. In this example, you spin-back slightly backwards, in order to catch him in the exposed ribs as he completes his punch.

Slightly retreating Spin-back Side Stop Kick against full-step Lunge Punch

The wisest use of this Stop Kick, and most others, is when you can lure your opponent into a predictable attack or counterattack by placing yourself in an unmistakable position he would not want to miss taking advantage of. A classic example of such a trap is the delivery of a full-momentum Straight-leg Roundhouse Kick to an opponent that tends to evade back and then counter. As your kick passes his evading midsection, you naturally start to present your back to his counterattack. He will not be able to resist that, but you have used the Roundhouse momentum to start your own Spin-back into a Side Stop Kick. The speed of your Spin-back and the amount of time you present your back to entrap him will be dependent on the circumstances and the relative proficiency of the protagonists. This combination should be seriously drilled by any fighter: It can be used as a trap as described, but also as a natural follow-up in case you did miss, un-purposely, with a Roundhouse that you expected would score.

Full-momentum *Muay Thai* 'Low Kick' turns into Spin-back Side Stop Kick

Typical application

This sequence shows the use of the kick against a jab. Being close to the opponent, the preferred version is very naturally a bent-over variation of the Spin-back Side Stop Kick. Follow up.

The Body-bent version of the Spin-back Side Stop Kick against a jab

The series below shows a variation preceded by a side step outside the centerline. As your opponent starts his rear-leg Front Kick, you step forward and in to evade the centerline while placing yourself in position for a faster and shorter spin-back. Make sure you deliver your Spin-back high Side Kick into his forward momentum. Follow up.

The Spin-back is preceded by a forward evading side step

Targets

Usually mid-body in order to stop the assailant's momentum: solar plexus, ribs, lower belly, hips and upper thigh.

The kick is very powerful, and therefore connecting with the chin, the throat, the armpit, and the general groin area will also stop the opponent.

Specific training

- Work with an attacking partner for timing and speed of Spin-back.

- Work for *power* on a swinging heavy bag which is now *thrown forcefully* by your partner, and not only left swinging. This must be a momentum-stopping kick, and you must get used to impact.

Self defense

These Figures show a high kick variation of this Stop Kick, against an opponent starting his own hopping front-leg Roundhouse Kick. Stop-kicking the head, when possible, is as effective as hitting the center of gravity! Catch him in the head in the midst of his hop, and follow up with a full powered Roundhouse Kick of your own; illustrated is a high Roundhouse follow-up, but you could as well kick his knee in a wise hi-lo combination.

High Spin-back Side Stop Kick

The Figures below show the use of the kick in its "*Hand-on-floor*" version and also targeting the *legs* of an aggressively punching assailant. Retreat half-a-step when attacked by a flurry of punches and spin-back while lowering your trunk and placing both head and upper body away from the attacks. Side-kick the assailant's front knee. Follow up, for example with another Spin-back Side Kick to the knee, with your other leg this time. You can then hound him as he retreats with further body-bent Side Kicks to the knees. A series of low Side Kicks is an extremely efficient self-defense follow-up: not only is the knee extremely vulnerable, but the Body-bent Side Kicks are difficult to deal with and are generally surprising to an untrained opponent. Also, do try to remember a general truth: if you have scored with something (in this case the Spin-back low Side Stop Kick), keep at it (further low Side Kicks); rare are the fighters who can learn from their mistakes on the spot, in the middle of the fight.

Low Spin-back Hand-on-floor Side Stop Kick followed by more low Side Kicks

But, again, the simplest tactics are generally the best. If your opponent is the type who tends to retreat when you kick in order to come back roaring with a counterpunch, then the next maneuver is a good way to handle him: stop-kick his counter. Tease him with a few Roundhouse Kicks to ascertain that it is indeed his bread-and-butter strategy. Then, deliver a powerful Straight-leg Roundhouse Kick—*Muay Thai*-style—in such a way that it will take you all the way into a Spin-back as the opponent evades back. As you pass him, he will start to come back forward for his Reverse Punch counter, hoping to catch you in your exposed back. But you have used the circular momentum to set up your own Spin-back Side Stop Kick that will catch him in the opening midsection.

Tactical trap: miss with a kick-through Roundhouse Kick in order to stop-kick his counter

Illustrative photos

The basic Essential
Spin-back Side Kick

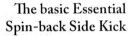

Classic Body-bent and Hand-on-floor versions of the Essential Side Kick

Spin-back Side Stop Kick in
free-fighting

**Far left: The Back version of the Spin-back
Side Stop Kick in free-fighting**

Left: Another Spin-back Side Stop Kick

Drilling the Essential Spin-back Side Kick

9. The Spin-back Back Stop Kick and other Back Stop Kicks

General

The basic Spin-back Back Kick is, in itself, mostly used as a Stop Kick. As mentioned in the previous section, it is a close relative of the Spin-back Side Stop Kick. It is even more powerful though, as a Back Kick is inherently more powerful than a corresponding Side Kick because of the muscles involved. It is also slightly faster, as the amount of spin-back required is smaller. This is the orthodox straight Stop Kick *par excellence*, which should break any forward momentum of the opponent. It can be delivered in place, slightly forward or slightly backwards, according to the situation and the range. Like all Back Kicks, it can be delivered in a regular *full* version or a **short** version, as described in previous work together with many more basic variations. Our previous book about *Essential Kicks* includes a full chapter about all possible basic Back Kicks.

Of course, one should always strive to deliver the Spin-back Back Stop Kick as early as possible in the attack process.

Key Points

It is imperative to be able to stop the *spinning* momentum, as soon as you get into position for the delivery of the *straight* back kick: If you do not, the kick will not strike the centerline but will go haywire. But remember that—in spite of being built of two different vectors—the kick is still one uninterrupted move! Refer to the theory of the basic Essential Spin-back Back Kick in previous work.

Targets

As it is a momentum-stopper, it aims for the mid-body, close to the center of gravity and usually left wide-open by the attack itself: Aim for ribs, solar plexus, lower belly, hips and general groin area.

For the very proficient, the throat and chin are also valuable targets.

Lean forward and in to evade a committed jab and execute the Spin-back *Short* Back Stop Kick

Description

The kick is simply a classic Spin-back Back Kick, as described in its Essential form in previous volumes, but is done to stop an attacking opponent. As mentioned, it can be delivered in the full or in the short version.

This sequence shows the execution, going slightly backwards, against a jab/cross combination.

The powerful Spin-back Back Stop Kick

Typical application

The Figures below show my kid brother's old favorite: Retreat widely once or twice from your opponent's attacks in order to build up his misplaced confidence. Be in control, but try to retreat just enough while giving a "bit of back" in a side stance. Your opponent will categorize you as a "flee-er" and unconsciously over-lunge in his futures attacks, all the while protecting himself less. You then suddenly stop-kick your emboldened opponent as you feel he prepares to lunge forward for his next attack. Follow up, with a back-fist for example. Even competitors who knew my brother's tricks were often lured into the well-laid trap, as it is an unconscious and innate process of confidence-building.

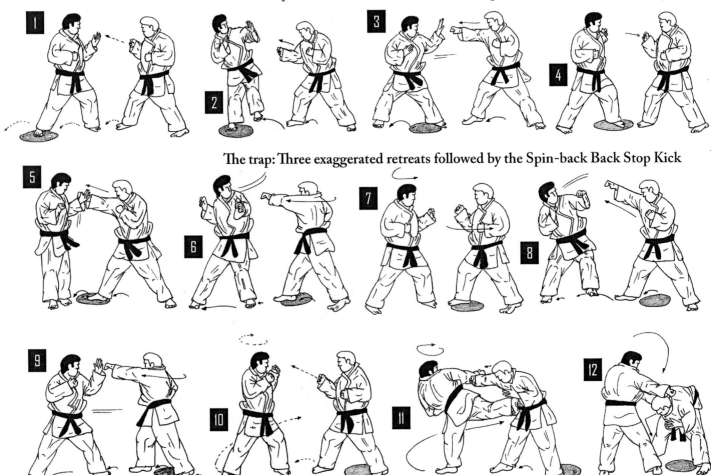

The trap: Three exaggerated retreats followed by the Spin-back Back Stop Kick

Specific training

- Drill the basic Essential Spin-back Back Kick, especially for a smooth transition from circular to straight momentum.

- Train for speed and accuracy on a swinging heavy bag.

- Train for power on a swinging heavy bag thrown forcefully at you by your partner.

- Train for all variations: at several ranges, in place, edging forward and backwards. Train for the *full* and for the *short* Back Kick.

- There is no alternative to drilling with a protected partner in light free-fighting!

Self defense

The series below shows the use of the kick against a jab, in a "*Sen-no-sen*" early delivery. Kick as soon as you 'feel' he is about to launch his own attack. Follow up by catching his extended hand *while* hitting the back of his neck with a ridge-hand strike (*Haito Uchi – Karatedo*) and reap up his front leg to throw him to the floor (*Uchi Mata – Judo*). Keep control of his hand and sit down into an underarm arm-lock control or all the way to an arm-break.

Preventive Spin-back Back Stop Kick at the start of a jab, followed by take-down and ground arm-lock

The Figures below show the use of the *short* kick, while *evading* the centerline, against a hopping front-leg Round-house Kick in opposite stances. Follow up with an Elbow Strike and a hopping front-leg Body-bent hooked Hook Kick behind the neck.

Short Spin-back Back Stop Kick out of the centerline

The same principles apply for any type of attack. This sequence shows the same *short* version of the kick delivered from out of the centerline, but this time against a full Lunge Punch. In a self-defense situation, it would be against a rush punch. Follow up with a preparatory Elbow Strike and an Outer Reap Throw (*O Soto Gari – Judo*). Finish him with a Stomp Kick to the ribs as he lands.

Angling *Short* Spin-back Back Stop Kick against step-punch

As mentioned before, all variations of the Back Kick are applicable in stop-kicking. As there is a full chapter about Back Kicks in the *Essential Book of Martial arts Kicks,* we shall limit ourselves to four examples, and first: a Spin-back *Uppercut* Back Stop Kick to the groin. Back-kicking the groin is always a good idea: even if you miss the testicles, the impact of a powerful Back Kick in the general area will always be very painful. The Figures that follow show the delivery of this Spin-back Stop Kick against an incoming assailant brandishing a stick. The assailant will expect you to retreat backwards and will plan his range accordingly. But, as an experienced Martial Artist, you know that the safest place against a wielding stick attack is *as close to him as possible*, with the added benefits of surprise and of foiling his range calculations. You deliver a *Short* Back Kick and do so *upwards* (*Essential* Uppercut Back Kick). Complete the Spin-back with an Elbow Strike and catch his head for a knee strike. Keep kicking until your assailant is fully vanquished, which is illustrated here by two additional Roundhouse Kicks.

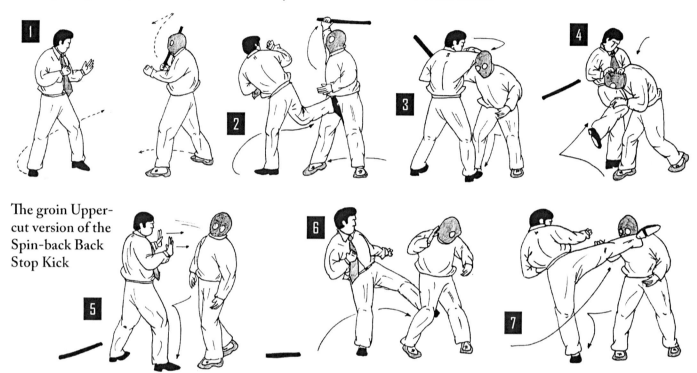

The groin Upper-cut version of the Spin-back Back Stop Kick

The second example is a *no-spin-back* version and a reminder that all kicks can be Stop Kicks. In this case, an Essential Hooking Back Kick is delivered to the groin of a kicking assailant while catching his kicking ankle. As your opponent starts delivering a classic Roundhouse Kick to your lower back, you evade forward and inwards while placing you rear hand in your back for a natural catch of his kicking leg. You kick his groin with a front-leg Upward Hooking Back Kick, and this will certainly lower his ankle into your waiting hand if it is not already there. The follow-up is even more painful: sit down on his extended knee and pull his ankle up!

Evading Hooking (no-spin) Back Stop Kick with leg catch

Third comes the *Short* version of the Spin-back Back Stop Kick, delivered simultaneously with a small side step and a ducking evasion. This is one smooth uninterrupted move against a committed jab in close combat.

Evading Spin-back *Short* Back Stop Kick

And last but certainly not least comes a Spin-back Short *Hooking* version of the Back Kick against a tackle attempt (or any maneuver that would give you control of the rear neck of a bent-over opponent). As your assailant plunges towards your legs, you retreat out of range and control the back of his neck when he tries to stand back up. Step forward and inside to start your Spin-back but keep control of his neck for as long as possible. Your Spin-back ends in an easy heel 'hooking' Back Kick to his offered face.

Spin-back Short *Hooking* Back Stop Kick against tackle attempt

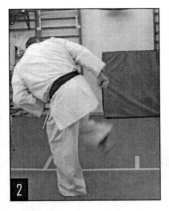

The classic Essential Spin-back Back Kick

Illustrative Photos

Left: The Body-bent version of the Essential Spin-back Back Kick

Right: The Essential Uppercut version of the Spin-back Back Kick

Illustrative Photos

The short version of the Essential Spin-back Back Kick – *Roy Faige* in an offensive combination

Respectively: the short, the very short and the ultra-short Back Kick

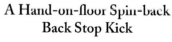

Offensive Essential Spin-back Back Kick after a first Back Kick

A Hand-on-floor Spin-back Back Stop Kick

The Essential Downward Back Kick is generally a Stop Kick

The Hands-on-floor version of the Spin-back Back Stop Kick

Illustrative Photos

Spin-back Back Stop Kicks in free-fighting

Spin-back Back Stop Kick in free-fighting – *Marc De Bremaeker*

The low Spin-back Back Kick is a great stop-kick too

The Flying Spin-back Back Kick is a great Stop Kick too

Groin Uppercut version of the Spin-back Back Stop Kick against a high kick

The Spin-back Upward Short Back Stop Kick in free-fighting against Axe Kick – *Roy Faige*

10. The Soccer Low Front Stop Kick

Mae sokutei osae uke (Karatedo), Jeet Tek (Wing Chung Kung Fu)

General

The Soccer Low Front Stop Kick is not a momentum-stopper, but it is an extremely disruptive kick that will stop any forward attack if caught early before it can fully develop. The kick is fast, easy to master, versatile and painful. If you had to choose only *one* kick to have to master for self-defense, this would be the one! Use it as soon as you detect your opponent's decision to lash out and focus fully on destroying his shin.

The Essential kick this Stop Kick derives from—called *Gedan Geri* in *Karatedo*—is well-known and very common in many arts, but it is often neglected because of its simplicity. I have a personal anecdote about it that should pique the reader's interest and that I usually tell when talking about the pernicious influence of the fighting rules of a given style. The rules of engagement for sport or controlled free-fighting in a given style will always influence the techniques and tactics used in the given style and taint them for real combat. A few examples follow. The hard *Kyokushinkai Karate* style does allow for full powered Roundhouse Kicks to the head but not for a jab to the face, resulting in a hard guard on both sides of the head but none for the face; how easy to jab such a fighter… Non- and semi-contact *Karate* tournaments used to mostly look like a pathetic exchange of body reverse-punching because of the points rules. *Tae Kwon Do's* sport kicks in tournaments lack power, as speed and scoring are more important. The beginnings of Full-contact Karate had a rule of 3 or 5 mandatory kicks per round, fast taken out of the way at the beginning of the round that from then on often became a simple boxing match. All these sports are respectable and efficient when mastered, but the rules of engagement changed their nature to allow sparring. Even MMA has its limiting rules! There is not much to do about it, as rules are needed, but *the modern and complete fighter should be able to fight in several rule frameworks, and should be conscious of the difference with the real world.*

And now for the promised anecdote: As a young, successful and cocky Semi- and Full-contact Karate fighter, I did take up *Savate-Boxe Francaise* in Brussels in the late Seventies. I was fast cut to size in free-fighting, and it was by the Soccer Low Front Stop Kick. There were no low kicks in Karate fights, and I was not used to taking them into account (Neither was the full Front Kick allowed then in *Savate* fighting). Each time I tried to kick or step forward, I had my kick or my step blocked by a fast Low Soccer Kick. Stop-kicking at its best! It took me several months of hurt pride and blue shins to reprogram my fighting to take that into account.

The Soccer Low Front Stop Kick is a fantastic weapon! The reader is invited to refer to previous work about *Low Kicks* for more information, relevant applications and additional examples.

Description

The reader is invited to refer to previous work for the description of this basic Essential Kick (*Gedan Geri – Karatedo*). The Stop Kick version, <u>*Mae sokutei osae uke (Karatedo)*</u>, is exactly the same kick but simply used to block (*Uke*) or immobilize (*Osae*). Always hit the closest target (the shin of the opponent's front leg). The Figure below shows the kick to the shin of a developing Front Kick. As it needs to be as powerful a kick as possible, it will nearly always be a *rear-leg* Stop Kick on your part. As will be shown in the applications, and because the kick is not a momentum-stopper, it is always wise to evade the centerline as soon as you have delivered the kick, and then to follow up obliquely.

In its Wing Chun version, the kick is more an obstruction or a precaution to be used while closing the distance: the leg is lifted straight into position with some back-leaning and then only is the body weight switched forward onto the opponent's knee or shin.

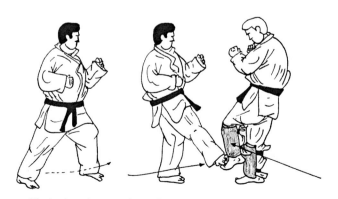

Kick the closest shin, drill with a *protected* partner

Key points

- As a Stop Kick, it must always be as powerful as possible, with the mindset of "crushing" the opponent's front shin.

- This is not a "slap" kick: you must kick one inch *into* the target before chambering back.

- Keep your guard up, as you are close to the opponent.

- Always follow up.

- The follow-up should optimally be while evading the centerline of the opponent's forward momentum.

Targets

Ankle, shin, knee.

The series below shows a "Stop the step" application, in opposite stances. Your opponent expects you to retreat—hopefully because you have conditioned him—and he develops a full-step Lunge Punch. As soon as his rear leg crosses forward, you stop-kick it and chamber back to lower the foot rearwards (where it was coming from) while pivoting with the hips out of the centerline. Using this same momentum, deliver a Hook Punch to the side of his head while controlling his hand. A natural follow-up would be a full-powered Roundhouse Kick to the head delivered from the side and coming straight to his face. The same leg can then deliver a Hook Kick to the back of his neck as he tumbles backwards.

Stop the step and follow up from the outside

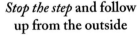

Typical application

We shall present here and later in the text, in turn, different flavors of this kick's use: Stop the kick, stop the step, stop the hop, stop the intention and stop the chamber…

The Figures below show a classic "Stop the kick" application. As your opponent develops his rear-leg Front Kick, you stop-kick the shin of his raising leg. Lower the kicking foot forward and *out of the centerline*, while controlling his front hand, and deliver a Palm Strike to his face. Follow up, for example, with a stepping-in circular Elbow Strike and a groin Knee Strike.

Stop the Front *Kick* and follow up

This sequence shows a "<u>Stop the hop</u>" application. As your opponent starts to hop forward for a front-leg Kick, you stop-kick his front lower leg as early as possible in the process. Keep your guard up, as the hopping move is often accompanied by a high Back-fist Strike or other hand move; block and control his hand or lean back if necessary. Once you have kicked into his momentum, he is basically at your mercy. The illustrated follow-up shows how you lower the kicking foot forward and out, while controlling his front shoulder. Continue with a full-powered Straight-leg Roundhouse ("Low kick") to the front of both his legs, at knee height; this should take him down *and* hurt his knees.

Stop the hop and take him down

The series below shows a "<u>Stop the intention</u>" application: you kick as soon as you *feel* that your opponent is going to start his attack. It takes practice—a lot—but is easier than it reads. Once your opponent's body has decided to attack, it will take it some time to rewire his brain to deal with your pre-emptive strike. In the example, you soccer-kick powerfully his front shin with a bent body; notice the hands stay down, as it is important to prevent any telegraphing (No upper body movement at all!). You can follow up with a rear-leg "Low Kick" and a groin Roundhouse as illustrated.

Specific training

- The best way to drill this kick as a Stop Kick is with a protected partner, moving and attacking (See page 91).

- Power and penetration of the Essential Kick itself must be drilled by hitting the heavy bag, the used tire, the medicine ball, and more… The kick must be a "dry" kick: fast, powerful and penetrating an inch or two before the chamber-back. Refer to previous work about drilling this basic Low Kick.

Self defense

These Figures illustrate the importance of the "bent-back" version of this kick. As your assailant launches a lunging jab, attack his front shin *while leaning back out of range*. Control the punch while lowering the kicking foot deep forward and *out of the centerline*. You are in perfect position for an Uppercut Punch to his exposed ribs, followed by a Roundhouse Kick to the groin or lower belly. The same leg can double up with a Stomping Side Kick to the knee (See our previous book about *Low Kicks*). You can finish the assailant up with a 'Low Kick takedown' or with an Outside Sweep (*Ko Soto Gari – Judo*).

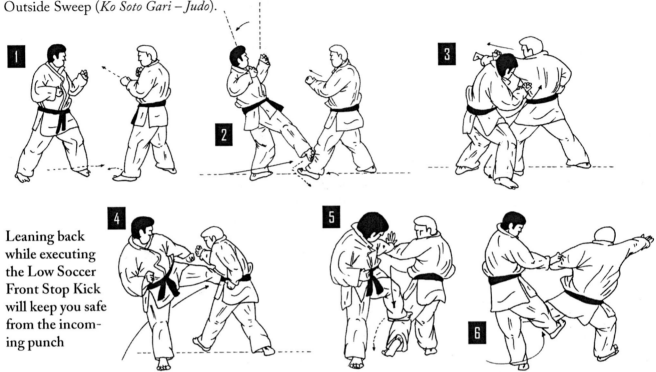

Leaning back while executing the Low Soccer Front Stop Kick will keep you safe from the incoming punch

This shows an example of "block-the-kick" at a very early stage of the chambering (basically: "*Stop the chamber*"). In fact, once your assailant is committed to a longer attack, it is best for you to get as close as possible to jam his technique. Rush him to stop-soccer-kick his own Front Kick as early as possible in its chambering. As you are then very close to him, follow up with a circular Elbow Strike as you land, followed by a powerful *Spin-back* circular Elbow Strike. You are in perfect position for an additional Knee Strike and a Straight-leg Roundhouse to his knee.

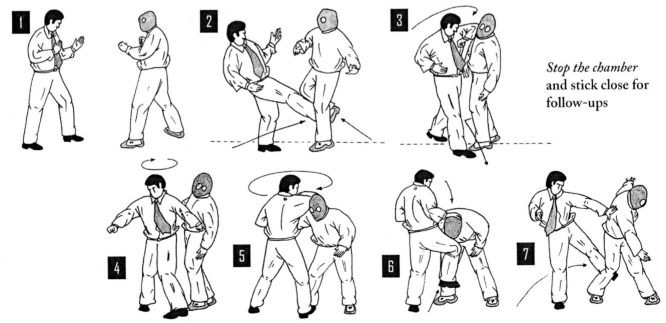

Stop the chamber **and stick close for follow-ups**

Our previous book about *Low Kicks* makes it very clear that Low Kicks like the *Soccer Low Front Kick* are excellent <u>Cutting Kicks</u>, and therefore Stop Kicks by definition. Many examples are given and the reader is invited to consult it. The book also makes clear that the applications of the Soccer version and of the *Regular* version of the Low Front Kick are interchangeable. Below comes a more complex example of a Cutting Stop Kick, which is executed simultaneously with a smothering catch. The version shown is that of the regular *classic* Low Front Kick (*Gedan Mae Geri – Karatedo*), though the Soccer version would be suitable too. In this example, your opponent has been identified as liking the painful Roundhouse Kick to the kidneys; as he predictably launches another one, you go slightly forward to prepare for the 'smother and catch' while starting your own Low Front Kick to the knee of his standing leg. Elbow-down his caught leg while chambering-back your kicking leg. You can, at this stage, twist violently to your inside in order to hurt his joint and get him to the ground. Proceed with a naturally-flowing classic Leg Lock. As illustrated, you can keep twisting down and add some neck-control to this very painful submission.

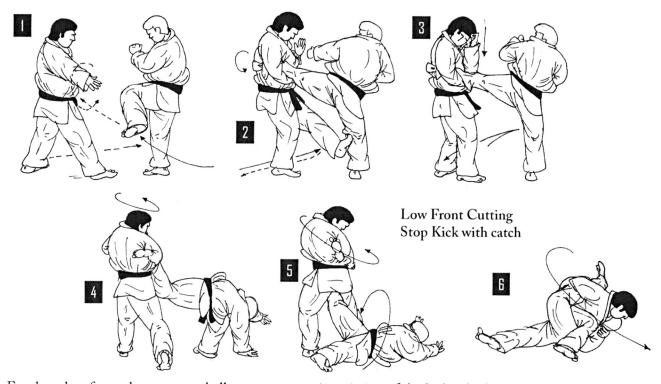

**Low Front Cutting
Stop Kick with catch**

For the sake of completeness, we shall present an exotic variation of the kick: a higher version targeting the ribs or the hip joint. This is a fast rear-leg Stop Kick found in some *Kung Fu* styles and that could be considered as a hybrid <u>short</u> version of the Essential *Outward-tilted Front kick*. It is a surprising kick but that requires timing, accuracy and a lot of training to be effective. It is presented here, against a full-step Lunge Punch, with an outside evasion and aimed at the opponent's ribs (opened by the punching action).

**Special hybrid Stop Kick between
high Soccer Front Kick and Outward-tilted Front Kick**

Examples of the Soccer Low Front
Stop Kick

Illustrative Photos

Stop-the-leg version of the
Soccer Kick against a Spin-
back Hook Kick

The classic Soccer Low Front Kick

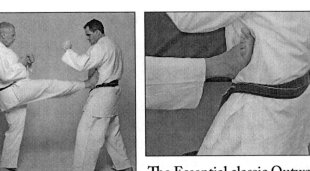

The Essential classic Outward-
tilted Front Kick

Soccer Low Front Stop Kick: stop the step-version

Soccer Low Front Stop Kick:
stop the kick-version

The high version of the Soccer Front Stop Kick

Illustrative Photos

Stop-the-spin by kicking the standing leg and follow up; Soccer Stop Kick against a Spin-back Hook Kick

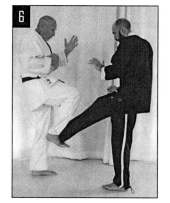

Fool me once, shame on me; fool me twice,... The second Front Kick is stopped by a Soccer Stop Kick

11. The Flying Side Stop Kick and other Straight Flying Stop Kicks

General

Flying kicks are in general good Stop Kicks because they carry inherently a situational change: when your opponent did decide to attack you were standing; in the middle of his attack development, you suddenly are in a higher plane! Note that the same analysis would hold truth for a Drop Kick, in which he would suddenly find you "lower". In our present case of Flying Kicks, not only are you now higher than planned for, but you also are coming towards him! In other words, the Flying Side Kick is a great momentum breaker: on top of being surprising, it is straight and has a very powerful forward momentum of its own which is backed by your whole body weight. But the other side of the coin for Jumping Kicks is that they are difficult *not* to telegraph and, therefore, that they are more suitable for attacking or stop-kicking from further away (out-range). They also need to always be fully committed; there is no going back. But, all in all, the Flying Side Kick is a great Stop Kick for the consummate flying kicker.

As a last word for this introduction, it is important to note that all what was and will be said about the Flying Side Stop Kick is true for all possible small variations of the Side Kick, as presented in previous work. Moreover, all will also be true for the flying versions of the other *Straight* Kicks, mainly the Front Kick and the Back Kick. All known small variations of the basic Flying Front Kick and Flying Back Kick can be used in the same manner and principles as Stop Kicks, with the same momentum-stopping benefits. The reader is invited to explore the possibilities on his own, based on the examples in this section.

**Low and long Flying Side Kick
by Ziv Faige**

Description

Refer to the description of the basic Flying Side Kick in previous volumes. The Stop Kick version is usually a "*jumping-up-from-both-feet*" variation of the Side Flying Kick, as illustrated below. Because of the importance of the relative range between the fighters in stop-kicking, remember to practice jumping in place, forwards and backwards when drilling the straight Flying Stop Kicks. The illustration at the top of page 99 shows the preferred *forward jump* as a Stop Kick. Please note, as mentioned at length in previous books, that Flying Kicks need not being necessarily high and spectacular; they can also be *long* and *low* (below left).

The "jumping-up from both feet simultaneously"-version of the front-leg Flying Side Kick

Forward-jumping Flying Side-Stop-Kick

Key points

Refer to previous volumes about the *Essential* Side Kick and the basic Flying Side Kick. All key points mentioned for good execution of these basic kicks are valid here. Especially important for Side Kicks are the chambering and the hip alignment during the kick.

Beware of the landing part: always land in guard and ready to follow up.

Specific training

- Perfect your Essential *Side Kick* and your basic *Flying Side Kick* techniques first and foremost. Flying kicks require a lot of practice. Refer to previous books about drilling those classic techniques.

- Drill all types against a swinging heavy bag (right). Mark the floor for range practice and jump forwards, backwards and in place from a whole array of different set-ups.

Targets

The head and the whole chest area. Preferably the *sternum* (Chest bone).

Stop-kick a heavy bag swung at you at random by a partner, from all possible ranges

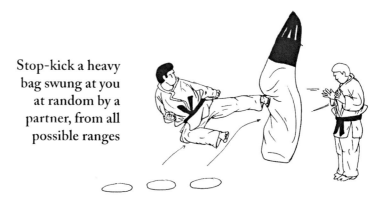

Typical application

The Figures that follow show a "jumping-back" version of the Flying Side Stop Kick against a classic full-stepped Lunge Punch.

Jump *back* and high into the Flying Side Stop Kick

The illustrations below show a "forward-jump" version *above* your opponent's developing Front Kick. Follow up with a powerful rear-leg Roundhouse as you land. The Photo shows such a stop-kick in the midst of its execution.

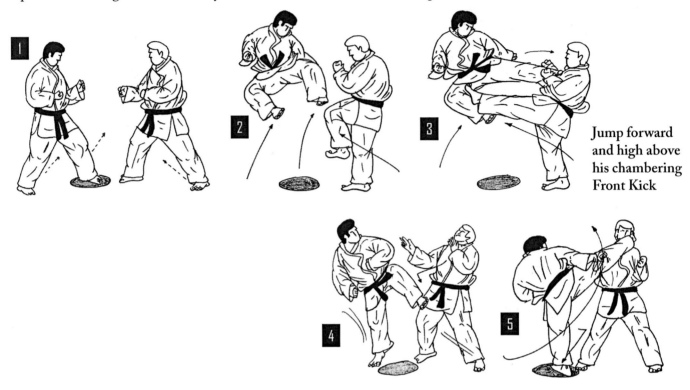

Jump forward and high above his chambering Front Kick

Illustrative photos

The Flying Side Stop Kick is generally a "jump-off-both-feet" version of the kick

Side Flying Kicks to the knee or hip are inherently Stop Kicks

Self defense

These Figures show a classic use of the kick against a sweep. You have noticed that your assailant tends to start his offensive combinations with an attempted sweep of your front foot. As he does so, jump up in place to avoid the sweep and cause him get somewhat off-balance. After the Flying Side Stop Kick, you could for instance land with a Hammer-fist Strike and follow further up.

Jump up in place to evade a sweep, and Side Stop-kick

As already mentioned, a Flying Kick needs not be necessarily aiming high. Flying Stop Kicks are also very efficient when targeting the hip, the thigh or even the knee. The Figures below show a pre-emptive Flying Side Stop Kick to the thigh of an assailant approaching menacingly. If you take the initiative unexpectedly, he will not be able to switch into defensive mode or accelerate his attacking move in time. Follow up.

Flying Side Stop Kick to the upper leg of an assailant as he approaches, but before he can strike you down

Illustrative photos

Vintage Flying Side Kicks, respectively by: Dotan De Bremaeker, Yannick Pierrard, Rui Monteiro, Marc De Bremaeker

12. The Flying Spin-back Outward Crescent Stop Kick

General

Circular Flying Stop Kicks cannot stop any serious forward momentum by themselves: they are very efficient 'timing' kicks aiming for the head, and executed while evading somewhat the incoming attack by fleeing upwards and slightly sideways in an unexpected change of plane. More specifically, the Flying Spin-back Outward Crescent Kick is a kick for close range-use, as the basic underlying Outward Crescent is not a long-range kick. In the most common use, the opponent expects you to retreat and is inclined to believe you are retreating as you start your spin-back. But, as he rushes forward committedly, you suddenly jump up while spinning back forward, and so disturb his plans and sense of distance. As mentioned, you usually aim at the assailant's head, but—as with all Crescent Kicks—you could be targeting his incoming limbs in 'Block Kick' fashion; a powerful circular kick to a joint is extremely devastating. Once mastered—and it takes quite a lot of training—the Flying Spin-back Outward Crescent Stop Kick is a surprisingly successful maneuver in its "*Sen–no–sen*" timing version. In any case, this is an important kick to drill for general kicking proficiency and for honing the ability to kick from any position and range.

Description

The kick is exactly as described in previous work about Flying Kicks. See the Figures at the bottom of this page, which depict the kick with the jump in place and slightly evading out. Execute the classic kick, but just make sure to time it to the first signs of your opponent getting into attacking mode.

The kick has the inherent advantage of being simultaneously a block: should you miss the opponent's head, your trajectory would still be blocking any straight attack.

Key points

- Refer to previous work; the kick is a classic kick, and generally used as a Stop Kick in most circumstances.

- The kick is best used coming towards the moving-in opponent's inside, to avoid the possible hindrance of his shoulder.

- The kick can only be delivered as a committed kick; once you have decided to go, there is no coming back.

Targets

The head nearly exclusively, from all sides. Eventually, the wrist, elbow, ankle and knee joints with *precision*.

Front view of the Flying Spin-back Outward Crescent Kick

Typical application

These Figures show the use of the kick as a timing move against a full-step Lunge Punch; as mentioned, it is preferable to target the inside of the punch.

Flying Spin-back Outward Crescent Stop Kick against Lunge Punch; jump slightly out of the center-line

Self defense

This series shows the use of the kick against a front-leg Roundhouse Kick attack, but this time, from the outside. The "both-feet-leave-the-ground-simultaneously" jump takes you deep out of the centerline and the line of attack. Start the kick early into his developing attack, and jump high to be able to deliver the Outside Crescent Kick over his developing (but jammed) Roundhouse Kick. This unorthodox delivery is more difficult to execute but more surprising as the kick comes from the opponent's blind side; it requires high jumping and angled delivery to be successful.

Specific training

• Master the basic kick first and foremost. Drill the grounded *Essential* basic Spin-back Outside Crescent Kick first. Then start to work on the hopping version, and then slowly and gradually to the Flying version. Refer to our book about Essential Kicks for drilling tips about Crescent Kicks.

• Work on the heavy bag

• Train with a head-protected partner.

• Flying Kicks require power and stamina. PLYO – FLEX training is highly recommended for fighting proficiency.

Illustrative Photos

The Essential Outside
Crescent Kick

The Essential
Spin-back Outside
Crescent Kick

 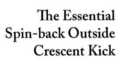 

The Flying Spin-
back Outside
Crescent Kick

13. The Flying Spin-back Hook Stop Kick

General

This is now the *longer-range* Flying circular Spin-back Stop Kick. The Flying Spin-back Hook Stop Kick has more reach than the previous Flying Spin-back Outside Crescent, and it is therefore a more classic counter to a Roundhouse Kick attack. This kick is also more powerful than the shorter corresponding Outside Crescent; enough so that is also effective if it hits the body. It is, though, more difficult to execute as it requires hip twist. As a Stop Kick, it is still generally an evasion kick though, as it cannot directly stop a forward momentum. It can be delivered jumping in place, forwards and backwards, but preferably while evading sideways. This spectacular kick is a favorite of many Tae Kwon Do tournaments, and very much iconic for this style.

Flying Spin-back away from the centerline: the key to Spin-back Circular Flying Stop Kicks

Description

The basic kick is described in previous work. Let it be noted that the Stop Kick-version is generally the "jumping-from-both-feet" variation, initiated as early as possible and aiming for the head. The power of the kick being derived from acceleration, it is a full-commitment kick. Tbe Figure below shows the delivery in place.

The Essential Flying Spin-back Hook Kick

Key points

- Refer to previous work about Spin-back Kicks and Flying Kicks. All key points are relevant to this Stop Kick-version. Especially remember that the spin-back starts with the head and the shoulders first, which will pull the hips and the leg.

- Jump high and always out of the centerline or the attack vector.

Targets

Preferably the head.

Because of its inherent power, secondary targets can also be considered by the proficient artist: between the shoulder blades, the kidneys, the chest bone and the solar plexus. This is generally not a Block Kick aiming at extending limbs.

The Figures below show the delivery jumping forward (and slightly off) against a full-step Lunge Punch.

Spin-back forward, high and to the opponent's inside; hook-kick into his punch

Typical application

This sequence shows the classic use against a rear-leg Roundhouse Kick attack, in opposite stances. Jump up as early as possible, forwards and towards the developing inside of the opponent. Follow up with a back-fist or hammer-fist strike as you land.

A classic Flying Stop Kick against the full Roundhouse

Specific training

A Spin-back Hook Stop Kick in free-fighting

- Always start your drills with the basic *grounded* Spin-back Hook Kick.

- Train to master the basic kick as such; stop-kicking will come later and naturally in free-fighting.

- When the basic kick is fully mastered, and only then, start working on jumping out of the centerline while spinning-back.

- Train on a static bag, making sure you start with an explosive jump up *with no tell-tales*. Use a mirror to check yourself.

- Use a medicine-ball on top of a standing bag as a target for your kicks. Concentrate on speed, precision and "kicking-through".

- Train with a head-protected partner faking realistic entries.

Self defense

This series show the use of the kick jumping in place (it could also be backwards) against a "Low Kick" to your inside front leg—in opposite stances. Follow up with a back-fist strike. To add insult to injury, you could follow up with another Spin-back Hook Kick from the same leg.

Evade a 'Low Kick' by jumping up and spinning back into a Stop Hook Kick

The sequence below shows the Stop Kick against an inside sweep attack in opposite stances. You jump up to evade the sweep and to deliver the Flying Spin-back Hook Kick as the opponent is off-balance from unexpectedly sweeping the void.

The jump-up is a sweep evasion turning into a kick

Should you be in same-stances, the technique can be delivered either after an evading leg switch, or by delivering the Spin Kick to his outside. (The *Switch Kicks* footwork is described in detail in our *Essential Book of Martial Arts Kicks*)

Switch feet in an overall slightly rearwards hop, then rebound on the floor for the Flying Spin-back Hook Stop Kick

The Flying Spin-back Hook Stop Kick can be as efficient when delivered from the opponent's outside

Illustrative photos

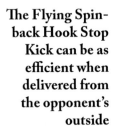

Left: Essential Flying Spin-back Hook Kicks

Below: The basic Essential Spin-back Hook Kick

14. The 'Timing' Hook Stop Kick and the Spin-back Hook Stop Kick

General

The 'timing' Hook Stop Kick used to be my *Tokui-waza* (Favorite technique) during my semi-contact tournament days, and one of the most effective kicks I know when delivered with good timing and technique: the developing kick is invisible during most of its trajectory, and often the surprise of the impact causes a knockdown or even knockout. This is certainly not a momentum-breaking technique, of course, and it must both be perfectly timed *and* target the head to be an effective Stop Kick. The results are, in my opinion, well worth the hard work and the risks. I cannot stress enough that it is a kick worth mastering. Although most of my usual opponents knew this kick was coming, I used to be able to score in most instances: this technique is *that* good, if you take the time and invest the effort to master it.

Remember that this is not a very powerful kick as there is no spin-back to gather energy: everything comes from your hips. The Stop Kick-version can be delivered in all possible variations of the Essential basic Hook Kick, as presented in previous work: hooking or regular, body-bent or straight, wide-arc or narrow…Experiment and choose what is best for your own physiognomy and mental attitude.

The *Spin-back* version of the kick is different but of particular importance, but the tactical uses and the principles involved are identical to what was presented in the previous section about the Flying Spin-back Hook Stop Kick. The principles of use and tactical situations are very different from those of the regular (no spin-back) Hook Kick. This (non-flying) *Spin-back* version of the Hook Kick is much more powerful than the regular basic kick, obviously because of the acceleration of the spin; but it also requires more time and forces you to present your back to the opponent. It is a great kick though, very typical of *Tae Kwon Do* and of *Sankukai Karatedo*.

The Spin-back Hook Stop Kick even stars in the codified exercises of traditional *Muay Thai Boran*, as "*Chorake Fad Hang*" ("The crocodile sweeps its tail"), in which an evaded typical *Muay Thai* kick-through Roundhouse Kick turns into a Spin-back Hook Kick as the opponent attempts to counter-attack. The first kick could be a feint or a miss, but the back offered to the opponent is definitely a trap to lure him into a counter that will be harshly stopped.

Two versions of the 'timing' front-leg Hook Stop Kick: body-bent hooking Kick and upheld-body/straight-leg Kick

The Spin-back version: *Mae Mai Muay Thai's Chorake Fad Hang*

Another example of the use of the Spin-back Hook Kick in a near-Stop Kick version is presented below. This is a check/catch/kick application against a regular Penetrating Front Kick that we present here in its *Yoseikan Budo* version for encyclopedic purposes. *Yoseikan Budo* is a syncretic Martial Art based on the "energy wave" principle that was founded by *Minoru Mochizuki* and which is very popular in Europe, and in France in particular. Master *Mochizuki* is special as he was a high-graded direct student of both *Jigoro Kano* and *Morihei Ueshiba*. In this version of a relatively well-known technique, the *Yoseikan* practitioner will retreat to control and scoop the incoming ankle, and then crouch while spinning back in order to place his own hips <u>below</u> the assailant's thigh. This variation will turn the following sweeping kick into a harsh takedown, as the fall for the opponent will start from a higher starting point. A very interesting technique in which you <u>kick</u> up and through.

High-takedown Spin-back Hook Cutting Kick against Front kick

Description

<u>The 'timing' version</u> is very simply a front-leg Hook Kick, generally hopping slightly forward towards the incoming opponent. Although it is best delivered so—with a slight forward thrust as soon as you "feel" the attack decision taking form in your opponent's mind—it can also technically be delivered *in place* or going slightly *backwards*.

The Figures that follow show the delivery in place against a jab at close range. In this example, you just lift the front leg into the Kick while leaning back away from the jab. A natural follow-up would be a Spin-back Short Back Kick to the exposed ribs (Hi – Lo combination).

Timing Hook Stop Kick, in place, against a jab; and followed by Spin-back Short Back Kick

And now, two "secrets":

1) You should be ready for the Stop Kick by having your front leg rather "<u>weightless</u>", but *without it being noticeable* by the opponent; this in itself takes some training and is as important as drilling the Kick. Being in guard with most my body weight on the rear leg without looking like it, is something I spent hours doing in front of the mirror, and then in free-fighting; this is one of the keys of the success of this stop-technique.

2) The other secret is the <u>trajectory</u> of the kick, keeping it out of the opponent's field of vision for as long as possible: very close to the opponent's body all the way up, and then taking some range out before impact a few inches into the target, as illustrated at right. This execution is what I call *ghost-kicking*, a lost art of dissimulation and misdirection in kicking that is applicable to many kicks and that will be the subject of a coming book. This 'ghost' delivery is less powerful than a classic wider arc, but it should be remembered that:

- knockouts come from surprise hits, not power;

- power can be improved *a lot* by serious drilling;

- you can always follow up if needed.

The sneaky 'ghost' trajectory of the Stealth Hook Stop Kick

Key points

- This is a Timing Kick, not to be delivered if you are not sure. It is a committed kick: no going back, no hesitation.

- The leg must climb up *close* to the opponent's body, so as to be in his blind spot for as long as possible. Hook in at the last second.

- Kick a few inches *into* the target and chamber back: this kick does not have the momentum to kick through (like the Spin-back version). The success is all about speed, accuracy and surprise.

- Always follow up if you have not achieved a knockdown.

- Bend the body away out of punching range if deemed by the circumstances.

Stealth Hook Stop Kick in tournament – *Marc De Bremaeker*

Targets

The head only, from all sides.

The Hook Stop Kick is a great technique to take down an opponent jumping into a flying kick or a jumping strike

Timing Hook Stop Kick in tournament – *Marc De Bremaeker*

Typical application

The Figures below aim to stress the fact that this is not a Straight Kick with stopping power and that it is sometimes preferable to evade a direct attack while kicking. In this example, you evade the jab first by bending backwards, and only then only do you deliver the Hook Kick. This is a "later-stage-timing" move, and not the ideal "nearly pre-emptive strike" presented earlier. This example is a same-stance application in which the kick is delivered from the opponent's outside, therefore requiring a "hooking" and higher Hook Kick.

Evade *back* first, then kick

This series makes the same point for a "later-stage timing"-version, but this time the evasion is sideways. You evade a full-step Lunge Punch by stepping out of the centerline first, and only then kicking. A great follow-up would be a rebounding same-leg Hook Kick, as a double-whammy.

Evade *out* first, then kick

Specific training

- This 'timing' kick deserves a lot of training. Start drilling the classic front-leg Hook Kick on the heavy bag, but concentrate on speed and on no-telegraph. Not on power.

- Then train on a swinging heavy bag; for speed and timing of impact. You can start concentrating on a bit of hip power.

- Train with a moving partner holding a focus pad or wearing a protective helmet, for timing and speed.

- Kick a swinging tennis ball for speed, timing and accuracy (See below right).

- Train for the *stealth* trajectory (See below):

  1. drill on the round-bottom bag. Lift the foot straight from below the bag and use the round bottom for the small out-move to gather momentum before impact.

  2. train by kicking a medicine ball from the top of a standing bag. Make sure you "shadow" the standing bag very close, and then try to kick the ball as far as possible *without kicking through* (just a few inches into the target).

Catch a swinging tennis ball with a Hook Kick

  3. exercise by kicking the heavy bag as powerfully as possible after lifting the leg all the way as close to the bag as possible.

Drilling the Hook Kick' stealth trajectory, with some power

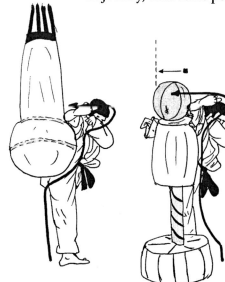

A 'timing' Hook Stop Kick

Self defense

In self-defense, always use the 'timing' kick as a pre-emptive strike, just as your attacker commits to his aggression. It will work even better if you have first conditioned your assailant to commit himself by retreating a few times from his attacks.

These Figures show the use of the "hand-on-floor"-version of the kick, hopping forward, as your assailant starts a rear-leg Front Kick. Follow up with a Back-fist Strike and a high Spin-back Back Kick (in, then out!). You could finalize with a takedown, like an inside thigh throw (*Uchi Mata – Judo*) for instance.

The disorienting "Hand-on-floor"-version of the 'timing' Hook Stop Kick

The series below shows the regular forward-hopping Hook Kick versus a hopping front-leg kicking opponent. Whether you opponent plans a Side Kick or a Roundhouse Kick, you hop forward into the kick as soon as he moves. You could follow up with a rear-leg full-powered "Low Kick" (Straight-leg Roundhouse) to the back of both his knees, in order to take him down to the ground.

The regular 'timing' Hook Stop Kick from the outside against a front-leg kicking assailant

The Figures that follow will show the kick in a tactical "Stop-the-counter"-version. After having gauged your assailant, you will provoke him into a punching counter which you shall then endeavor to stop-kick. Launch a convincing reverse punching-fake, but stop it as soon as it provokes a reaction. You can then spin the hips back and start your front-leg stealth Hook Stop Kick, bending away from his one-two punching reaction. You could follow up by turning the lowering leg into an Outer Reap throw (*O Soto Gari – Judo*).

Fake an attack to provoke an expected counter that you will proceed to stop-kick

There are, of course, many variations of the Hook Kick; all versions can be adapted to stop-kicking. Just to whet the reader's appetite, we shall present a Small Inside-version of the Stop Hook Kick delivered to a kicking opponent's calf. This is an evading Cutting Kick and not a sweep: you must kick hard into the calf muscle. As your assailant delivers a telegraphed rear-leg Front Kick, you evade out and catch the incoming leg *while* hopping into the front-leg Small Inside Hook Kick. This is a 'timing' Stop Kick that will both hurt him and get him on the ground. Your evading catch of his kicking leg has placed you in preparatory position for a painful ankle lock; make sure you control his leg strongly by squeezing it between your knees and let yourself go down. Arch your back to press his Achilles tendon in this classic ankle lock.

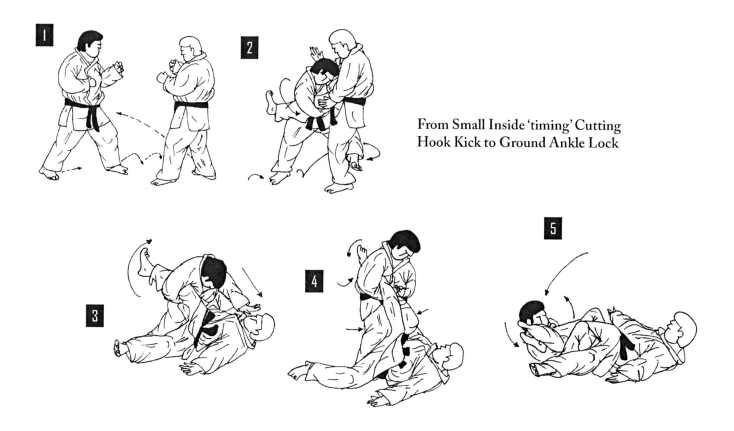

From Small Inside 'timing' Cutting Hook Kick to Ground Ankle Lock

Illustrative Photos

Two versions of the Hook Kick: Body-bent and Hand-on-floor

Timing drill on swinging heavy bag

An evading rear-leg Hook Stop Kick

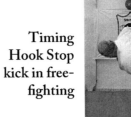

Timing Hook Stop kick in free-fighting

Timing Hook Stop Kick in free-fighting

The Hook Stop Kick can be used from very close

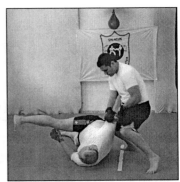

Following up on a 'timing' Hook Stop Kick

15. The Blocking Crescent Stop Kick and other Crescent Kicks

General

This is the most classic limb-blocking Stop Kick, although it can also be used as a regular "timing" Stop Kick as well. The Crescent Kick is a fast and very powerful kick and it can be very painful when used against the joint an incoming limb. It is not a momentum-stopper though, and it will usually be used from further away: it will generally be a rear-leg Kick aiming—not at the incoming body—but at the preceding attack limb. That is why it is usually used with some nimble footwork, like the half-step backwards or the legs-switching. The reader should note that the Crescent Kick is a very common kick in traditional *Karate* forms (*katas*), where it is nearly always followed by a Side Stomp Kick. This wide representation in *Katas* says a lot about its old-days realistic efficiency.

Rear-leg Crescent Stop kick to thigh of developing Roundhouse

All what will be said in this section is widely valid for the blocking *Outside Crescent* Stop Kick that will not be described as a separate section: all principles are the same and the experienced artist will have no difficulty in devising his own variations and drills. The reader is also invited to refer to the *Leg Blocks* examples presented in the introductory sections of this book.

Crescent Stop Kick to incoming punch

Description

This is very simply an *Essential* basic Crescent Kick used in a Stop-kicking context. The Figures below show the *classic* use, against a full-step Lunge Punch. This example is starting from opposite stances, but the kick is the same from same-stance relative positions; it would just be striking the inside of the elbow instead of its outside. As your opponent starts his punch, you retreat half-a-step with the front leg and launch a powerful Crescent Kick aimed at the elbow joint. In your mind, this should be a *kick to the joint*, not a block! In an uninterrupted move, you chamber somewhat and naturally Stomp-kick his front foot. You can follow up with a Back-fist Strike. [The all-important Stomp Kick is described in detail in our previous book *Low Kicks*]. This classic drill is, in my opinion, a bit contrived: the stepping Lunge Punch starts from an unrealistic distance, and the kick is partly a Leg Block to a punch that would never have reached its target anyway. The drill is still an important starting point though, as it is teaching the principles of stop-kicking, of range appreciation, of timing and of precision targeting. As the neophyte fighter improves, the punch could become a shorter lunging Jab, and the kick would be delivered after a longer retreating half-step.

The old classical Crescent Kick-to-Side Stomp maneuver

A more realistic use of this rear-leg Crescent Stop Kick would be a 'timing' Kick will full forward commitment as the opponent starts his stepping punch: you meet him unexpectedly half-way and aim for his head; your kicking leg itself still works as a *secondary* block of the developing punch (See below).

The more modern 'timing' version of the rear-leg Crescent Stop Kick

Key points

- This is a kick first, and a block only far second: you have to concentrate on causing pain at the targeted *joint*. The blocking and displacing the attacking limb is a secondary benefit.

- Always chamber back somewhat by bending the leg after impact: it adds fizz to the impact.

- Always follow up, preferably from the chambered back position.

Targets

- Attacking the incoming leg: the knee from all sides, the sides of the thigh, the hip, the shin, the lower calf and the ankle from all sides.

- Attacking the incoming arm: the wrist, elbow, forearm and upper arm from all sides; the shoulder and the fingers of an open hand.

- As a regular stop-kick: the head, the solar plexus area, between the shoulder blades, the kidneys and the general groin area.

Typical application

This shows an atypical application of the kick, as a front-leg Block Kick when quite close to the opponent. As your opponent hops forwards for a front-leg Roundhouse Kick, you retract your front leg *with a small step rearwards* and then use the (now) front leg to attack his rising knee. Follow immediately with a Jab/Cross combination as he will be off-balance; and then eventually with a full powered rear-leg Roundhouse Kick to the neck to finish him off (eventually adjusting distance, again). The half- or full-step retreat, followed by a front-leg Stop Kick is a fantastic maneuver to adjust distance while stop-kicking; but remember that it requires a lot of training to be able to impart power to front-leg Kicks. The Crescent Stop Kick is certainly no exception, and training will do you good; do not ever think that you "know" a technique and do not need to drill it!

On the other hand, here is also the time to remind the reader that—should extra power be required from the front leg—*switching* legs by hopping in place (or while adjusting slightly) is the way to go. Switch Kicks for power are at the heart of stop-kicking.

Front-leg Crescent Stop Kick after back step

Specific training

- Drill the basic Essential Crescent and Outside Crescent Kicks.

- Drill for speed, timing and accuracy *first* (no power!) with a padded partner.

- When the kick is well-mastered as a Stop Kick, work for power on the still and swinging heavy bag.

- Power development for the Crescent Kicks should be heavily based on Plyo-Flex training.

Self defense

The "blocking" application being classic and straightforward, we will show here another interesting and atypical application: An evading "timing" Stop Kick to the head with no limb-blocking at all! The Figures below show how you lunge *forward* against a Spin-back Hook Kick, as close as possible to the rotation axis of your assailant. You can then Crescent-kick his head with full power as he completes his target-less Spin-back Kick. Push him down and punch the back of his head. Should you be a ground-fighter, you are now in ideal position to "get" his back.

Timing Crescent Stop Kick after getting close to the opponent

The series below shows an example of a front-leg Crescent Block Kick in a complex technique against a *provoked* counter. Against an opponent who is himself prone to stop-kicking, you *feint* a forward move. As he starts developing his own Side Pushing Stop Kick, you lean back while lifting your front leg and catching his over-reaching kicking foot. Your front-leg Inside Crescent Kick will block his natural incoming jab and move his caught leg. The follow-up is a dangerous technique to be drilled carefully: Your Crescent Kick goes down over his caught leg; as if that has not caused enough joint damage, you can now sit on his knee while pulling his ankle up. Do this slowly in training and violently in a real-life self-defense situation.

Front-leg Crescent Block Kick with leg catch, followed by knee break

Should you want a more easy-to-control finish to the technique, you could choose to ease into a classic ankle/knee/hip Twisting Lock instead of sitting on his knee; the Leg Lock is as dangerous, but it is easier to control and to use as a more ethical invite to submission.

The alternative Leg-lock conclusion to the same stop/catch technique

One will often find treatises in which the Crescent Kicks are used to attack arms yielding weapons, like knives, sticks or—God forbid—even guns. Although such kicks could be of interest in some very very specific instances, and still at great risk, the author wants to take his distance from such maneuvers. Kicking a gun or a knife out of the hands of an assailant is more an old James Bond movie stunt than an advisable technique. It is dubious that a kick will easily disarm, and any miss would result in placing the kicker in an extremely vulnerable situation: That much should be clear to the experienced artist.

In spite of all this, we shall present two examples of stop-kicking an assailant's arm holding a stick. The reason is two-fold:

- A wielded stick is a less dangerous weapon, especially once you get closer to the assailant where the kinetic energy of the stick is neutralized.

- As mentioned in the introduction, the drilling of techniques does not mean they will be used in sport or in real combat: it allows your body to practice and internalize a whole range of scenarios from the banal to the extreme; in combat, the body is on auto-pilot and will use instinctively what is best. This is why you train hard and why you try a whole array of different techniques.

This illustrates a rear-leg Crescent Stop Kick to the elbow of an incoming stick arm. In this example, your assailant comes menacingly from out of range while wielding his stick; you go forward to confront him and kick. You can follow up with a naturally flowing Side Kick to his knee. This is a good drill for timing and precision, in spite of being slightly unrealistic.

Crescent Stop Kick against stick attack; target the outer elbow joint

Should you execute—in the same situation—the Crescent Stop Kick to the inside of the stick arm, as illustrated by the sequence below, you would feel safer: the closer you get to the assailant, the better; and you should aim for the head. In case you miss the head, you would still get the arm. The natural follow-up of the technique would also be a Side Kick to the knee. You could conclude with a Spin-back Outside Crescent Kick.

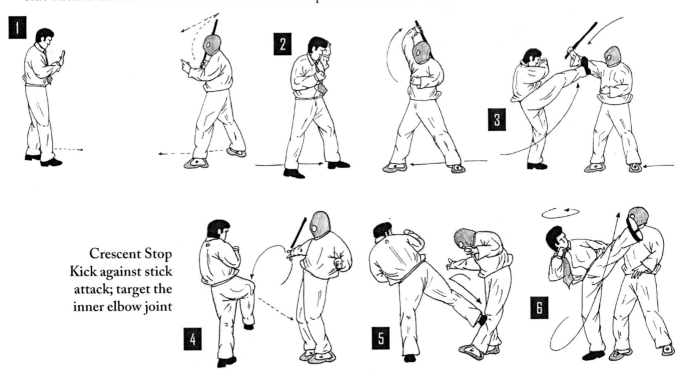

Crescent Stop Kick against stick attack; target the inner elbow joint

For the sake of completeness, we shall present an example based on the *Outside* Crescent Stop Kick. As mentioned, all principles are the same as for the regular (Inside) Crescent Kick discussed in depth in the section. This example is, again, a limb attack, although the use of the Kick is more of a "kick-everything-in-its-passage": if not the limb, the head. The Figures below show a threatening assailant who suddenly initiates a flurry of punches, punches that you will avoid by retreating fast while protecting yourself as best as you can. As soon as you have cleared the danger zone, deliver the front-leg Outside Crescent Kick that will both hurt him and stop the next developing punch, or even that will catch him in the head. You can very naturally follow with a fully-hipped Hook Punch, and reverse the hip twist for a powerful Palm Strike to the chin. Keep hitting him; for example with a low Soccer Front Kick to the shin as he tumbles back.

The Outside Crescent Stop Kick

Last, but certainly not least, we shall present an interesting example of the Downward Heel Stop Kick, in an Outward Crescent trajectory. This is a sophisticated Kick that is neither for the beginner, nor for the faint-hearted. But it is certainly a valid maneuver for the flexible and advanced Artist; it is more easy to use in free-fighting than it may seem and it is a very efficient technique when successful. I strongly recommend its practice, as it can open the horizons of many fighters and emphasize the broad range of surprising techniques that is available to the advanced student. In the example below, you block an incoming high Roundhouse Kick with a very high Outside Crescent Block Kick that, from its apex, turns into a Downward Heel Kick (*Axe Kick*) to the attacking leg. The Axe Kick is quite damaging to the joints and will also place the assailant off-balance. You can easily follow-up as he struggles to retain his balance and composure, with a high Roundhouse for instance.

This is also the right place to note that the Downward Heel Kick can be, in itself, a very good 'timing' Stop Kick for the fast and flexible.

Downward Heel Stop Kick to an incoming Roundhouse Kick

Illustrative Photos

Crescent Stop Kicks

Illustrative Photos

The Crescent Stop Kick can be delivered from very close, as soon as you feel an attack decision taking form in your assailant's mind

The basic Essential Crescent Kick attacking the guard

Outside Crescent Stop Kicks

The classic Essential Outside Crescent Kick attacking the guard

16. The Shin Front Pushing Kick

Te Khrung Khang Khrung Khow (Muay Thai)

General

The Shin Front Pushing Kick is a very important small Kick for close combat fighting, like *Muay Thai* or *MMA* for example. It is very much in use in Thai boxing to keep the opponent at a distance and also to prevent clinching. You simply hit your opponent's midsection, pushing forward, with the shin of your Roundhouse-like chambered leg. It is not a devastating kick, but still painful, if aiming explosively at the floating ribs, the hip joint or the upper thigh. It is a must-practice kick, especially if you want to avoid clinching, in-fighting and wrestling situations. Once you have mastered the basic maneuver, you should then drill the Kick seriously to learn to deliver maximum power to the lower ribs of the opponent and make it the punishing technique it can be.

Description

The Figure at left below shows the classic rear-leg delivery: raise the leg as if delivering a Small Roundhouse Kick, but without extending the leg. Simultaneously, push the hip forward, with a hop if necessary, to hit his mid-body with the shin. If the opponent is in forward momentum himself, he should add this energy to that of your kick at impact.

The kick can also be delivered, less powerfully, with the front leg, with or without a hop forward.

The very useful *Te Khrung Khang Khrung Khow*

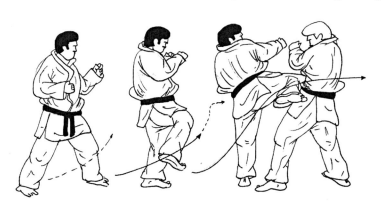

The rear-leg Shin Front Pushing Kick to the ribs

The hopping front-leg Shin Front Pushing Kick to the upper thigh

Key points

- Keep your guard up as you are very close to your opponent.

- Keep your upper body as immobile as possible when starting the kick, to avoid telegraphing.

- The power of the kick comes from the <u>hip thrust</u> (and eventual forward hop).

- Concentrate on making this a painful kick and not a simple push-away.

- Aim for a few inches *into* the target.

- There is no chamber back, as the kick's power comes from the hip thrust; just lower the leg.

- *Always* follow up!

Drilling the Shin Front Push Kick for power and penetration

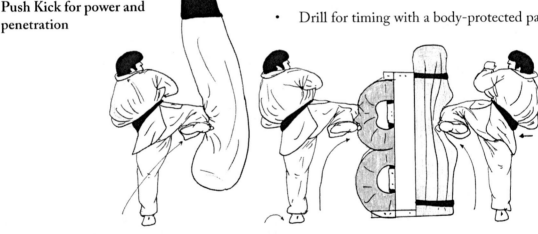

Targets

As a pushing away stop-kick: anywhere at mid-body, close to the opponent's center of gravity from solar plexus to upper thigh.

To make it as painful as possible, you should aim for the lower floating ribs or the forward hip joint.

Specific training

- Drill for form, power and hip push on the heavy bag, the old tire or the padded wall (See below). Drilling for explosive power delivery is important and will make this kick a redoubtable secret weapon.

- Work on the swinging bag, thrown by a partner, for stopping-power and for timing. Drill all variations: front leg, rear leg and hopping.

- Work with a moving partner who will be trying to push you away with a training shield.

- Drill for timing with a body-protected partner.

Illustrative Photos

The sneaky but so effective Essential Outward groin Ghost Kick

Typical application

The Figures below show the use of the kick as a "timing" Kick against a Jab. Follow up with a Reverse Punch. And then maybe a Crescent Kick…

Timing Shin Front Pushing Kick at the hint of a Jab

The Figure that follows shows an interesting offensive application of this special kick. This is not a pure Stop Kick per se, but somewhat of a sneaky Feint Kick. It will be presented here though, as the delivery is the same as the basic Stop Kick. In a clinch position, your opponent will probably expect Knee Strikes, *Muay Thai*-style. For good measure, you can deliver a preparatory knee strike or two. You then go through the obvious motions of preparing another Knee Strike: pulling his neck down, pushing him back and pulling your hips away. You start the delivery, but at the last possible moment, you smoothly switch to an unexpected Shin Front Push Kick to his hip joint (or to the front of his thigh). Follow up.

Use the Shin Front Push Kick to the hip joint when in clinch position

Self defense

These Figures show the use of the kick to pre-empt a "Low Kick" (Straight-leg low Roundhouse Kick). As your assailant has revealed himself to be keen on "Low Kick" attacks to your inner front knee, you avoid one or two of those and then wait for the next one. Most fighters do not change tactics in mid-fight and will keep repeating the same openings, combinations and attacks. As you discern the start of a new "Low Kick", you will hop forward with an aggressive Shin Front Push Kick to the hip joint. As he is off-balance but still very close, you must "stick" to him with immediate follow-ups, like full-hipped circular Elbow Strikes. You can conclude with the sneaky and decisive Outward Ghost Kick to the groin.

Front-leg hopping Shin Front Pushing Kick to jam the start of a "Low Kick

The last example will be the simple stopping of a Reverse Punch, but with the purpose of emphasizing the follow-up. As this Stop Kick takes you close to the opponent, a natural follow-up would be the use of powerful elbow strikes, as already encountered. And, in fact, the Shin Front Pushing Kick is very common in *Muay Thai*, where Elbow Strikes are bread-and-butter fare. In the example below, your assailant's Cross Punch is stopped with a Shin Front Pushing Kick coupled with the additional safety of a block or at least some arm control. The Stop Kick is then followed by a whirlwind of vicious Elbow Strikes. More and/or other elbow strikes could have been presented, but the illustrations below give the reader an idea of the possibilities and invite him to look for his own preferences.

A natural synergy: the Shin Pushing Front Kick and Elbow Strikes

17.   The Half-drop Side Kick

General

We have *not* presented in this book about Stop Kicks any of the relevant Ground Kicks or *Drop Kicks*, even those already presented in previous work. The author thinks that it would be unnecessary doubling up that would lengthen this book with no purpose. As mentioned in the Introduction and throughout the text, *all* kicks can be used as Stop Kicks. This is just the frame of mind that makes them Stop Kicks. Referring to all kicks here, would make it tedious and unnecessarily repetitive. *Drop Kicks* especially, can be, and are generally used as Stop Kicks. Those are "change of plane" techniques, just like Flying Stop Kicks: Your attacker is hitting in a plane from where you disappear—in the case of Drop Kicks —down! Many examples are presented as applications in our book about *Essential Kicks* to which you are invited to refer.

We will just present here one hybrid kick, something between a *Hand-on-floor Side Kick* and a *Drop Back Kick*. It is delivered this way for reasons of speed, timing and distance. It will be clear to the skilled practitioner, that all variations between those two basic kicks are valid, according to the situation, your specific physiology and your preferences. Just remember that the Half-drop Side Kick is a maneuver against high attacks only. If you are a ground-kicker or a ground fighter, this Stop Kick is a great way to go down to the ground.

For reference, we shall make use of this section to present a few Essential Drop Kicks in the *Illustrative Photos* section.

The Half-drop Back Side Stop Kick

Description

The illustration below shows how you bend and twist down as soon as your opponent's attack takes form; you place both hands on the floor and start chambering. You do not "fall" all the way onto your knee like for a full Drop Kick, but you deliver the Back-Side Kick directly as your hands reach the floor. The floor base gives this Kick power and the forward momentum of the attacker tends to "impale" him on your Kick.

The Half-drop Side Kick

Key points

- This is one flowing uninterrupted movement: Twisting down rearwards on your hands and kicking.

- Keep your eyes on the opponent and always follow up.

- This is a 'timing' technique, in spite of being a Straight Stop Kick.

Targets

Preferably aim for his exposed ribs or his groin.

The hip joint, the solar plexus and even the knee are also relevant targets.

Typical application

The Figures below show the use of the Kick against an opponent fond of a Jab/Cross /Rear-leg high Roundhouse Kick-combination. You could follow up with a Double Drop Back Kick.

The Half-drop Side Stop Kick

Specific training

- Practice this kick for *speed* of execution and timing, against the heavy bag *swung* powerfully by a partner (See page 129).

- Drill *timing* with a free-fighting partner

Self defense

This shows the use of the kick in a situation where it is important to have your upper body as far away as possible from your attacker, like a knife threat. As your assailant gets close while brandishing and poking his knife around, you time the Half-drop Side Stop Kick to catch a step or a poke of his. Once committed, do not stop but keep kicking in a 'Hand-on-floor' or at least 'Body-bent' position. Deliver multiple kicks at his *knee* and *groin* until he gets on the defensive or even drops his weapon. Although I would not advise it on a clean professional knife attack, the Body-bent Kicks are an excellent and relatively unexpected offensive defense against knife threats; you can inflict damage while presenting a very difficult target to deal with, and your aggressive attitude will send most thugs go look for easier prey.

The Half-drop Side Stop Kick keeps your upper body away from weapons and other danger

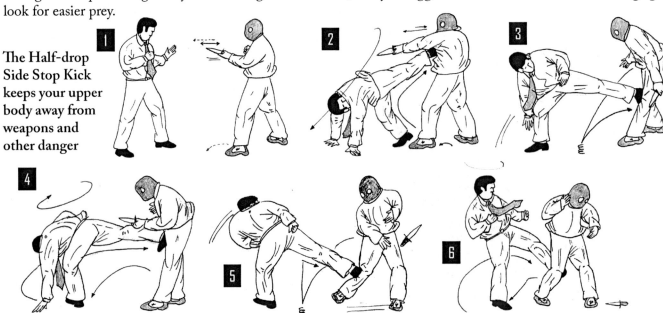

Illustrative photos

The Downward Back Kick:
Hand-on-floor and a great Stop Kick

The Back-version of the Half-drop
Side Stop Kick

The *Drop* Twin Roundhouse Kick

Hand-on-floor Kicks: respectively Side Kick and Roundhouse Kick

Drop Spin-back Hook Kick

The *Drop* Front Stop Kick

Illustrative photos

The *Drop*
Roundhouse Kick

The *Drop*
Side Kick

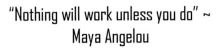

"Nothing will work unless you do" ~
Maya Angelou

The *Drop* Hook Kick

Illustrative photos

The classical *Drop* Back Kick

The Essential *Drop* Twin Back
Kick, a powerful Stop Kick too

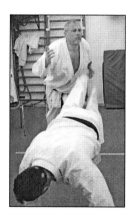 

The good fighters of old first put themselves
beyond the possibility of defeat, and then waited
for an opportunity of defeating the enemy.
~ Sun Tzu

Afterword

We have come to the end of our overview of the main Stop Kicks. As mentioned several times in the text, all possible Kicks can be and are potentially Stop Kicks: Any kick delivered to stop an attack—even at the very beginning of your opponent's crystallizing decision to attack—is by definition a Stop Kick. We have tried to present the most commonly used Stop Kicks and to illustrate the little variations to basic kicks that will make them more suitable for stop-kicking.

We did consider, at the start of this work, the possibility of organizing the Stop Kicks into categories; we finally decided against it because of the fluidity of the distinctions between Stop Kicks and, again, because of the fact that all other Kicks could be Stop Kicks too. The categories we did consider were along the following lines: *Pushing Kicks* (Like the Front Pushing Stop Kick), *Momentum-stopping Kicks* (like the powerful Spin-back Back Kick), *Timing Kicks* (like the 'timing' Roundhouse Stop Kick), *Momentum-gathering Circular Stop Kicks* (like the Spin-back Hook Kick) and evading kicks. But these categories do not cover all kicks mentioned and some Kicks belong to several categories at the same time.

Therefore, the author decided to describe the Stop Kicks in an order more or less related to how often-encountered these particular Stop Kicks are. This is by no means an objective classification; nor is it a classification by descending importance. The Front Pushing Stop Kick is very common, but not very damaging: it is used mostly to keep an opponent away. The 'timing' Hook Stop Kick, found much lower down the list, is not seen that often but it is so efficient that it has become the author's favorite technique.

The reader can, from our point of view, consider the order of the kicks' presentation as random, without missing any point we intended to make in this body of work.

Here are, at random, a few more Essential kicking maneuvers that could be called Stop Kicks; the list is certainly not exhaustive.

Flying Side Stop Kick to the hip

The Low Front Stop Kick

The Front Stop Kick

'Cutting' Stop Kicks

Mid-level Roundhouse Stop Kick

Attempted
Spin-back
Hook Stop
Kick in free-
fighting

Groin Stop Kicks:
Upward Side Kick and
Front Lift Kick

Spin-back Back Stop Kick in free-
fighting – *Marc De Bremaeker*

The Essential Drop Overhead Back Stop Kick

Cutting Drop Side Stop Kick
– *Roy Faige*

The Essential Outward Ghost Stop Kick

The Cutting Drop Spin-back Hook Stop Kick – *Ziv Faige*

"The five S's of sports training are: stamina, speed, strength, skill, and spirit; but the greatest of these is spirit."
– Ken Doherty

Stop-kicking is more a matter of the mind; and training for Stop Kicks is therefore more trying to acquire a mindset. Progress will come with trying in free-fighting and then trying in more demanding circumstances, like sport tournaments and the like. As mentioned, the 'timing' Hook Stop Kick has long been my preferred fighting technique, but it had not always been so. In fact, beforehand, I used to stop-kick in sport events with the front-leg hopping Roundhouse Kick or sometimes with its Downward-version. I did drill many other possible Stop Kicks in training though, until one day, my body on autopilot decided to launch a Stop Hook Kick in a tournament. The point is simple: nobody does tactical thinking in the middle of a stressful fight; the body works on its own, feeding on muscle memory and on the intuition built on hours of training and free-fighting. You must drill Stop Kicks of all types, even if they do not "feel" right for you at the beginning. After hours of training, which in any case does not ever go to waste, your body will "feel" which is the automatic 'right' technique for a certain situation.

So try the Kicks presented here. Try your own variations. Once you have got the principle right, try your own preferred Kicks as Stop Kicks. Then try them in free-fighting, there is no shame in failing at the first attempts. Then, you will certainly get there. Stop-kicking is probably the most effective and sophisticated way to kick, as you catch your opponent *at his most vulnerable*; it is well worth the effort.

Back Stop Kick

All questions, comments, additional techniques, special or vintage photos are welcomed by the author and would be introduced with credit in future editions. Just email: martialartkicks@gmail.com

The author is trying to build a complete series of work that, once finished, could become an encyclopedic base of the whole of the Martial arts-Kicking realm, a base on which others could build and add their own experiences.

Any comment, addition, vintage photograph, anecdote or suggestion is welcome: martialartkicks@gmail.com

In his endeavors the author has already penned:

The Essential Book of Martial Arts Kicks – Tuttle Publishing (2010)

Plyo-Flex Training for Explosive Martial Arts Kicks – Turtle Press (2013)

Low Kicks - Advanced Martial Arts Kicks for Attacking the Lower Gates – Turtle Press (2013)

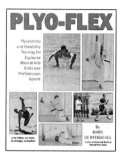
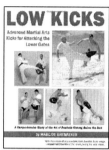
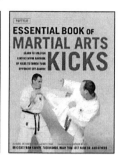

In the same frame of mind, the following works are in preparation:

Flying Kicks

Ground Kicks

Feint Kicks

Recommended Reading relevant to this book:

Timing in the Fighting Arts by Loren W. Christensen and Wim Demeere (Turtle Press)

Warrior Speed by Ted Weimann (Turtle Press)

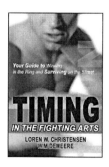

Also Available from Turtle Press:

Plyo-Flex
The Art of Joint Locking
Muay Thai Fighting Strategies
Introduction to Tien shan Pai
Modified Wing Chun
Juji Gatame Encyclopedia
Survivalist Kung Fu
Explosive Muay Thai
Fight Back
Drills for Grapplers
Winning on the Mat
Wrestle and Win
Fighting the Pain Resistant Attacker
Total Defense
Conditioning for Combat Sports
Kung Fu Grappling
Street Stoppers:
Sendo-Ryu Karate-do
Power Breathing
Throws and Takedowns
Vital Point Strikes
Groundfighting Pins and Breakdowns
Defensive Tactics
Secrets of Unarmed Gun Defenses
Point Blank Gun Defenses
Security Operations
Ultimate Fitness through Martial Arts
Complete Kicking

Low Kicks
Triangle Chokes
Vital Leglocks
Boxing: Advanced Tactics and Strategies
Grappler's Guide to Strangles and Chokes
The Armlock Encyclopedia
Championship Sambo
Complete Taekwondo Poomse
Martial Arts Injury Care and Prevention
Timing for Martial Arts
Strength and Power Training
Complete Kickboxing
Ultimate Flexibility
Boxing: A 12 Week Course
The Fighter's Body: An Owner's Manual
The Science of Takedowns, Throws and Grappling for
Self-defense
Fighting Science
Martial Arts Instructor's Desk Reference
Solo Training
Solo Training 2
Fighter's Fact Book
Conceptual Self-defense
Martial Arts After 40
Warrior Speed
The Martial Arts Training Diary for Kids
Teaching Martial Arts
Combat Strategy
Ultimate Kung Fu Drills

For more information:
Turtle Press
http://www.turtlepress.com

CPSIA information can be obtained
at www.ICGtesting.com
Printed in the USA
FFOW02n0459170414
4885FF